MY CAVE LIFE

IN

VICKSBURG

WITH

LETTERS OF TRIAL AND TRAVEL

By Mrs. Jas. M. Loughborough

THE REPRINT COMPANY, PUBLISHERS
Spartanburg, South Carolina
1976

This volume was reproduced from an 1882 edition in
The Mississippi Collection, University of
Mississippi Library, Oxford,
Mississippi.

Reprinted: 1976
The Reprint Company, Publishers
Spartanburg, South Carolina

ISBN 0-87152-217-9
Library of Congress Catalog Card Number: 75-46574
Manufactured in the United States of America on long-life paper.

Library of Congress Cataloging in Publication Data

Loughborough, Mary Ann Webster, 1836-1887.
   My cave life in Vicksburg, with letters of trial and travel.

    Reprint of the 1882 ed. published by Kellogg Print Co., Little Rock, Ark.
    1. Vicksburg, Miss.,—Siege, 1863—Personal narratives. 2. Loughborough, Mary Ann Webster, 1836-1887. I. Title.
E475.27.L88   1976   973.7'344'0924   75-46574
ISBN 0-87152-217-9

Mr. Edward King, of New York, author of Scribner's "Great South" article, in writing of "Cave Life in Vicksburg," says: "It is a charming little book, fresh and vivid as a photograph."

The author of "Living Female Writers of the South," says of "Cave Life in Vicksburg:" "A sprightly and well-written book, full of graphic and interesting pictures of scenes within the city of Vicksburg during the siege."

The St. Louis Republican, in 1864, says, in a review of "Cave Life in Vicksburg:" "This is one of the books coming out of the great war, that is worthy of all acceptation. The author tells her plain, unvarnished story, in such a simple and truthful manner, that one can see vividly the scenes depicted."

MY CAVE LIFE IN VICKSBURG.

MY CAVE LIFE

IN

VICKSBURG.

WITH

LETTERS OF TRIAL AND TRAVEL.

By Mrs. Jas. M. Loughborough.

PUBLISHED BY
D. APPLETON & CO.,
1864.

REPRINTED BY
KELLOGG PRINTING COMPANY,
LITTLE ROCK, ARK.
1882.

Entered, according to Act of Congress, in the year 1864, by
D. APPLETON AND COMPANY,
In the Clerk's Office of the District Court of the United States for the Southern District of New York.

TO ONE

WHO, THOUGH ABSENT, IS EVER PRESENT,

THIS LITTLE WAIF

IS TENDERLY AND AFFECTIONATELY

Dedicated.

CONTENTS.

CHAPTER	PAGE
I. Our Party set out for Vicksburg — The Ride and Scenery—Scenes during the first Bombardment—View of the City and River—Opening of a Battery—The Enemy, ...	9
II. At Night the Signal Gun sounds—The Gunboats are coming down—The Town Awake—Shell Music—The Boats near us—Rapid Descent to the Cave—They have passed safely—Why the Confederate Guns do not fire—The Burning Transport, . . .	15
III. Masked Battery on the Opposite Shore—Taking the Cars—Fright of the Negro Porters—Major Watts's Party—Stampede of Ladies, ...	20
IV. Jackson threatened—Colonel Grierson—General Pemberton departs—My Mind is made up to go also—Ride on the Cars—Vicksburg again, . . .	25
V. To Vicksburg again—Aspirations—Troops passing to Black River—General Pemberton orders all Non-Combatants to leave the City, ...	29
VI. Rumors of the Federal Advance on Black River—Gunboats on the River—Cannonading and Fire at Warrenton — General Pemberton's Forces engaged at Black River, ...	35
VII. Sunday, the 17th—After Church—The Demoralized Army—Soldiers' Stories, ...	40
VIII. Fresh Troops from Warrenton for the Intrenchments—"We'll Protect You"—Fears, ...	46
IX. The Ball in Motion—View from the Court House—Federal Prisoners sent across the River—Movements of Gunboats, ...	49

CONTENTS.

CHAPTER		PAGE
X.	Groundless Fear of an Attack by Gunboats—Shells fall—The Bombardment begins—Cave Shelter—Garrison Force—Cave and Cave Life,	55
XI.	Buried Alive—House Breaking—Appearance of Shell at Night—Under the Root of a Fig Tree,	63
XII.	Fire at Night—A Narrow Escape—Moonlight—Shells from the Battle Field—Employment and Traffic,	69
XIII.	Shells from the Rear of the City—Providential Deliverance—Pantomime—Pea Meal—Hospital Accident,	73
XIV.	Dogs—Horses—Descent of a Shell through a Cave—A Mother's Cries—Deserted Homes—Silence,	78
XV.	An Excitement—Sinking of the Cincinnati—Sky Parlor Hill—Moving Prospects,	84
XVI.	Fall of a Shell at the Corner of my Cave—Music—Casualties of the Day,	89
XVII.	Ride to the Fortifications—Number of Caves along the Road—Appearance of the New Home—Change of Missiles,	94
XVIII.	Morning—Charge of General Burbridge—Horrors of War—An Important Discovery,	99
XIX.	An Acceptable Present—Hunger—Half Rations—In the Rifle Pits,	105
XX.	A Rainy Morning—A Waterspout—Dismal Experience—Brighter Prospects—An Unfortunate Sleeper,	109
XXI.	Weary—The Couriers from General Johnston—Dangerous Pasturage—Mule Meat—Local Songs—Missed by a Minié Ball,	114
XXII.	A Wounded Horse—Shrapnell Shells—Charge on the Intrenchments—Fearful Firing,	122
XXIII.	An Unhappy Accident—The Unfortunate Ladies of Vicksburg—Approach of Mortar Shells near the Intrenchments,	128
XXIV.	Death of a Faithful Servant—Blowing up of a Fort—Loss of Prominent Officers—Surrender of Vicksburg,	135
XXV.	A Fright—George my Protector—A Polite Soldier gets the Tent Fly,	143
LETTERS OF TRIAL AND TRAVEL,		147

PREFACE.

NOT being permitted to pass the lines with the paroled prisoners, who, without arms or accoutrements, set out, after the surrender, on their sad march to Mobile, the author of "Cave Life in Vicksburg" proceeded to St. Louis. There, one evening, in conversation with a friend who had been reading her little journal of the siege, the thought was suggested of publication. On writing to Appleton & Co. regarding the matter, a reply was received requesting the transmission of the manuscript journal; and the author was urged to dispatch the papers as speedily as possible while public interest in the siege life was still vivid.

The book was then published (in 1864) with but little delay. While it is a compilation of notes hastily put together by a then, unpracticed writer; it is also a little bit of veracious history. This history, with its short-comings, was credited to a Herald or Tribune—which, I have forgotten—reporter, by a book reviewer upon the staff of the New York Independent. The reviewer asserted that the style of the book was assumed; and affirmed that the writer had not left his newspaper office during the siege.

At one time the authoress designed re-writing the book, but the copy-plates having been purchased and presented to her, it was deemed hardly advisable to get out new plates for an altered second edition.

Now, in 1881, on getting out a second edition, the authoress desires to express her grateful appreciation of the kindness with which the edition of 1864 was received. She wishes to express to the officers and soldiers of the Confederate army at Vicksburg her acknowledgement of the gentle services and courtesy that contributed to her comfort and welfare as the sad days there passed on.

Words cannot express the wonder and admiration excited in her mind by the conduct of those brave men at Vicksburg; how they endured with unflinching courage, the shower of ball and shell; how they confronted the foe with undaunted resolution, closing the ranks steadily as their comrades fell by hundreds about them; how they endured, with steadfast perseverance, the hunger, the wet, the privation; firmly facing the fact before them —that they were, day by day, fighting against overpowering odds; and when the forlorn hope wavered and the flag was pulled down, how the dauntless faces paled before defeat as they had never paled before a foe.

The second edition, like the first, is dedicated to M——, to one then absent—now gone before —reverently and tenderly—to a memory.

MARY W. LOUGHBOROUGH.

Little Rock, Ark, Jan. 1, 1882.

MY CAVE LIFE IN VICKSBURG.

CHAPTER I.

OUR PARTY SET OUT FOR VICKSBURG—THE RIDE AND SCENERY—SCENES DURING THE FIRST BOMBARDMENT—VIEW OF THE CITY AND RIVER—OPENING OF A BATTERY—THE ENEMY.

IT has been said that the peasants of the Campagna, in their semi-annual visits to the Pontine marshes, arrive piping and dancing; but it is seldom they return in the same merry mood, the malaria fever being sure to affect them more or less. Although I did not leave Jackson on the night of the 15th piping and dancing, yet it was with a very happy heart and very little foreboding of evil that I set off with a party of friends for a pleasant visit to Vicksburg. Like the peasants, I returned more serious and with a dismal experience. How little do we know with what rapidity our feelings may change! We had been planning a visit to Vicksburg for some weeks, and anticipating pleasure in meeting our friends. How gladly, in a few days, we left it, with the explosions of bombs still sounding in our ears! How beautiful was this evening: the sun glowed and warmed into mellow tints over the rough forest trees; over the long moss that swung in slow and stately dignity, like old-time dancers, scorning the quick and tripping movements of the present day! Glowing and warming over all, this evening sun, this mellow, pleasant light, breaking in warm tints over the rugged ground of the plantation, showing us the home scenes as we passed; the sober and motherly cows going home for the evening's milking through the long lanes between the fields, where the fences threw shadows across the road; making strange, weird figures of the young colts' shadows, lean and long-limbed and distorted; the mothers, tired of eating the grass that grew so profusely, were standing in quiet contentment, or drank from the clear runs of water. And so we passed on by the houses, where the planter sat on his veranda, listening to the voice of his daughter reading the latest paper, while round her fair head, like a halo, the lingering beams of the sun played.

And on to Black River, " Big Black," with its slow, sluggish tide! Dark, like the Stygian stream, it flowed in the mist of the evening, the twilight. And soon we see Vicksburg, classic ground forever in America. The Hudson must now yield the palm to the Father of Waters. Our interest will centre around spots hallowed by the deeds of our countrymen. I had thought, during the first bombardment of Vicksburg, that the town must have been a ruin; yet very little damage has been done, though very few houses are without evidence of the first trial of metal. One, I saw, with a hole through the window; behind was one of corresponding size through the panel of the door, which happened to be open. The corner of the piano had been taken off, and on through the wall the shot passed; one, also, passed through another house, making a huge gap through the chimney. And yet the inhabitants live in their homes (those who have not lost some loved one) happy and contented, not knowing what moment the house may be rent over their heads by the explosion of a shell.

" Ah!" said I to a friend, " how is it possible

you live here?" "After one is accustomed to the change," she answered, "we do not mind it; but becoming accustomed, that is the trial." I was reminded of the poor man in an infected district who was met by a traveller and asked, "How do you live here?" "Sir, we die," was the laconic reply. And this is becoming accustomed. I looked over this beautiful landscape, and in the distance plainly saw the Federal transports lying quietly at their anchorage. Was it a dream? Could I believe that over this smiling scene, in the bright April morning, the blight of civil warfare lay like a pall?—lay over the fearful homesteads—some, even now, jarred by the shock of former conflicts—lay by the hearthstones, making moan in many a bereaved heart looking forward with vague fears to the coming summer.

What soul in the land but has felt and witnessed this grief—this unavailing sorrow for the brave and untimely dead? I thought of the letter from the sorrowing one in Iowa, whose son, a prisoner, I had nursed, receiving with the last breath words for the distant, unconscious mother; of her sorrow in writing of him in his distant grave; of her pride in him, her only son. How many in the land could take her hand and weep over a mutual sorrow! And in the hospital wards, men, who still hold the name of Americans, together were talking of battles, prisoners, and captors, when each told the other of acts of bravery performed on hostile fields, and took out pictures of innocent babes, little children, and wives, to show each other, all feeling a sympathy and interest in the unknown faces. Verily, war is a species of passionate insanity. While standing and thinking thus, the loud booming of the guns in the water batteries startled me, the smoke showing that it was the battery just below me, that opened, I was told, on what was thought to be a masked battery on the opposite shore. No reply was elicited, however; and on looking through the glass, we saw in the line of levee, between the river and the Federal canal, a spot where new earth seemed to have been thrown up, and branches of trees to have been laid quite regularly in one place. This was all. General Lee, however, had ordered the spot to be fired on, and the firing continued some little time. Our ride that evening had been delightful. We sat long on the veranda in the pleasant air, with the soft melody and rich swell of music from the band floating around us, while ever and anon my eye sought the bend of the river, two miles beyond, where the Federal transports, brought out in bold relief by the waning, crimson light of the evening, lay in seeming quiet. Still, resting in Vicksburg seemed like resting near a volcano.

CHAPTER II.

AT NIGHT THE SIGNAL GUN SOUNDS—THE GUNBOATS ARE COMING DOWN—THE TOWN AWAKE—SHELL MUSIC—THE BOATS NEAR US—RAPID DESCENT TO THE CAVE—THEY HAVE PASSED SAFELY—WHY THE CONFEDERATE GUNS DO NOT FIRE—THE BURNING TRANSPORT.

At night I was sleeping profoundly, when the deep boom of the signal cannon startled and awoke me. Another followed, and I sprang from my bed, drew on my slippers and robe, and went out on the veranda. Our friends were already there. The river was illuminated by large fires on the bank, and we could discern plainly the huge, black masses floating down with the current, now and then belching forth fire from their sides, followed by the loud report, and we could hear the shells exploding in the upper part of town. The night was one of pitchy darkness; and as they neared the glare thrown upon the river from the large fires, the gunboats could be plainly seen. Each one, on passing the track of the brilliant light on the water, became a target for the land batteries. We could hear the gallop, in the darkness, of couriers upon the paved streets; we could hear the voices of the soldiers on the riverside. The rapid firing from the boats, the roar of the Confederate batteries, and, above all, the screaming, booming sound of the shells, as they exploded in the air and around the city, made at once a new and fearful scene to me. The boats were rapidly nearing the lower batteries, and the shells were beginning to fly unpleasantly near. My heart beat quickly as the flashes of light from the portholes seemed facing us. Some of the gentlemen urged the ladies to go down into the cave at the back of the house: M— insisted on my going, if alone. While I hesitated, fearing to remain, yet wishing still to witness the termination of the engagement, a shell exploded near the side of the house. Fear instantly decided me, and I ran, guided by one of the ladies, who pointed down the steep slope of the hill, and left me to run back for a shawl. While I was considering the best way of descending the hill, another shell exploded near the foot, and, ceasing to hesitate, I flew down, half sliding and running. Before I had reached the mouth of the cave, two more exploded on the side of the hill near me. Breathless and terrified, I found the entrance and ran in, having left one of my slippers on the hillside.

I found two or three of our friends had already sought refuge under the earth; and we had not been there long before we were joined by the remainder of the party, who reported the boats opposite the house. As I had again become perfectly calm and collected, I was sorry to find myself slightly fluttered and in a state of rapid heart-beatings, as shell after shell fell in the valley below us, exploding with a loud, rumbling noise, perfectly deafening. The cave was an excavation in the earth the size of a large room, high enough for the tallest person to stand perfectly erect, provided with comfortable seats, and altogether quite a large and habitable abode (compared with some of the caves in the city), were it not for the dampness and the constant contact with the soft earthy walls. We had remained but a short time, when one of the gentlemen came down to tell us that all danger was over, and that we might witness a beautiful sight by going upon the hill, as one of the transports had been fired by a shell, and was slowly floating down as it burned.

We returned to the house, and from the veranda looked on the burning boat, the only one, so far as we could ascertain, that had been injured, the other boats having all passed successfully by the city. We remained on the veranda an hour or more, the gentlemen speculating on the result of the successful run by the batteries. All were astonished and chagrined. It was found that very few of the Confederate guns had been discharged at all. Several reasons had been assigned; the real one was supposed to have been the quality of the fuses that were recently sent from Richmond, and had not been tried since their arrival. This night of all others they were found to be defective. The lurid glare from the burning boat fell in red and amber light upon the house, the veranda, and the animated faces turned toward the river—lighting the white magnolias, paling the pink crape myrtles, and bringing out in bright distinctness the railing of the terrace, where drooped in fragrant wreaths the clustering passion vine: fair and beautiful, but false, the crimson, wavering light.

I sat and gazed upon the burning wreck of what an hour ago had thronged with human life;

with men whose mothers had this very night prayed for them; with men whose wives tearfully hovered over little beds, kissing each tender, sleeping lid for the absent one. Had this night made them orphans? Did this smooth, deceitful current of the glowing waters glide over forms loved and lost to the faithful ones at home? O mother and wife! ye will pray and smile on, until the terrible tidings come: "Lost at Vicksburg!" Lost at Vicksburg! In how many a heart the name for years will lie like a brand!—lie until the warm heart and tried soul shall be at peace forever.

CHAPTER III.

MASKED BATTERY ON THE OPPOSITE SHORE—TAKING THE CARS—FRIGHT OF THE NEGRO PORTERS—MAJOR WATTS'S PARTY—STAMPEDE OF LADIES.

AT breakfast, on the morning of the 17th, we heard discussed the question, Whether there was a masked battery on the opposite shore or not? After some words on the subject, pro and con, we ranged the shore with the glass, seeing what the gentlemen believed to be a battery. They had been talking some moments, when I took the glass and saw a number of Federal soldiers walking on the levee toward the spot where the battery was supposed to be. Several others seemed to be engaged on this very place removing the branches. I called one of the gentlemen to look. I had given up the glass but a few moments, when a volume of smoke burst from the embankment, and two shells were sent, one after the other, exploding at the depot just below us. It was indeed a battery, with two guns, which commenced playing on the city vigorously.

We were to leave that morning, and hearing that the cars would not venture up to the depot, went to a point below, where we found many anxious persons awaiting their arrival. We entered the cars, and were sitting quite securely and comfortably, when it was whispered around, much to the consternation of passengers, that they were ordered to approach the depot as near as possible, and take on freight; and thus we were carried up, under shelter of a high bluff, with many misgivings on my part, as shell after shell exploded on the hill above us. A nervous gentleman leaned forward and told me that we were in great danger, and, speaking in the same manner to many of the ladies, suggested that, if we made the request, the conductor would doubtless back into a safe place.

Although so frightened, his mode of relief was so evidently selfish that the gentlemen began joking him most unmercifully. In looking out of the window, although I felt a sympathy for the poor fellow, I could not but be amused at the ludicrous scene that presented itself: the porters bring

ened and trembling. Fortunately a gentleman friend, discovering their absence, overtook, and proceeded with them. As a shell would be heard coming, he would cry, "Fall!" and down they would drop in the dust, party dresses and all, lying until the explosion took place; then up, with wild eyes and fiercely beating hearts, flying with all speed onward. After running about a mile in the fewest moments possible, and falling several times, they stopped at the first house, and remained until their friends sent out for them in carriages.

"If you could have seen our party dresses when we reached home, and our hair, and the flowers, full of dust, you would never have forgotten us," cried one. "Ah!" said another, "we laugh gayly this morning, for we are leaving the guns behind us; but last night it was a serious business, and we absolutely ran for our lives." How delighted I was with the quiet rest of our home in Jackson! I mentally forswore Vicksburg during the war. But man proposes, and God disposes."

CHAPTER IV.

JACKSON THREATENED—COLONEL GRIERSON—GENERAL PEMBERTON DEPARTS—MY MIND IS MADE UP TO GO ALSO—RIDE ON THE CARS—VICKSBURG AGAIN.

OUR quiet was destined to be of short duration. We were startled one morning by hearing that Colonel Grierson, of the Federal army, was advancing on Jackson. The citizens applied to General Pemberton to protect them. He answered that there was no danger. Suddenly, the ladies' carriage and saddle horses were pressed, and the clerks and young men of the town were mounted on them, and started out to protect us (!). I was told that the first time they met the Federal troops most of them were captured, and we heard of them no more. We need not have feared, for Colonel Grierson was spoken of everywhere (so some ladies from the district through which he passed, afterward told me) as a gentleman who would not allow his men to treat any one with the slightest disrespect, or take the least article from a citizen's house; and they all treated ladies courteously. There was not one instance of unkindness to any human being, so far as I could learn. He should have the thanks of every brave man and Southern woman. This man, though an avowed enemy, scorned to torture or wage war on God's weaker creation.

Again the rumor came that from Canton a large Federal force was advancing on Jackson. Jackson was to be defended!! which I doubted. Soon General Pemberton left and went to Vicksburg—Mrs. Pemberton to Mobile. Batteries were being erected in different parts of the town—one directly opposite the house I was in. I stood considering one morning where it was best to go, and what it was best to do, when a quick gallop sounded on the drive, and a friend rode hastily up and said, " Are you going to leave ? " " Yes," I answered, " but I have not yet decided where to go." " Well, I assure you there is no time for deliberation; I shall take my family to Vicksburg, as the safest place, and, if you will place yourself under my charge, I will see you safely to your husband." So the matter was agreed upon, and we were to leave that evening. Still, I was in doubt; the Federal army was spreading all over the country, and I feared to remain where I was. Yet I thought, may I not be in danger in Vicksburg? Suppose the gunboats should make an attack? Still, it was true, as my friend had said, we were in far more danger here from the rabble that usually followed a large army, and who might plunder, insult, and rob us. No; to Vicksburg we must go!

Very hurriedly we made our arrangements, packing with scarcely a moment to lose, not stopping to discuss our sudden move and the alarming news. Our friends, also, were in as great a panic and dismay as ourselves. Mrs. A. had some chests of heavy silver. Many of the pieces were such that it would have taken some time to bury them. Her husband was absent, and she feared to trust the negro men with the secret. Another friend feared to bury her diamonds, thinking in that case she might never see them more; feared, also, to retain them, lest, through negroes' tales, the cupidity of the soldiers might become excited, and she be a sufferer in consequence. Every tumult in the town caused us to fly to the doors and windows, fearing a surprise at any time; and not only ladies, with pale faces and anxious eyes, met us at every turn, but gentlemen of anti-military dispositions were running hither and thither, with carpet bags and little valises, seeking conveyances, determined to find a safe place, if one could be found, where the sound of a gun or the smell of powder might never disturb them any more; and, as they ran, each had an alarming report to circulate; so that with the rush and roar of dray, wagon, and carriage, the distracting reports of the rapid advance of the Federal army, and the stifling clouds of dust that arose—with all, we were in a fair way to believe ourselves any being or object but ourselves.

The depot was crowded with crushing and elbowing human beings, swaying to and fro—baggage being thrown hither and thither—horses wild with fright, and negroes with confusion; and so we found ourselves in a car, amid the living stream that flowed and surged along—seeking the Mobile cars—seeking the Vicksburg cars—seeking anything to bear them away from the threatened and fast depopulating town.

CHAPTER V.

TO VICKSBURG AGAIN—ASPIRATIONS—TROOPS PASSING TO BLACK RIVER—GENERAL PEMBERTON ORDERS ALL NON-COMBATANTS TO LEAVE THE CITY.

LEAVING the threatened, teeming town behind us, we moved slowly on—our friends, my little one, and myself—toward Vicksburg. Ah! Vicksburg, our city of refuge, the last to yield thou wilt be; and within thy homes we will not fear the footstep of the victorious army, but rest in safety amid thy hills! and those whom we love so dearly will comfort and sustain us in our frightened and panic-stricken condition—will laugh away our woman's fears, and lighten our hearts from the dread and suffering we have experienced. Yet, is there any place where one is perfectly safe in these terrible times? As we travelled along,. the night air blowing so refreshingly upon us through the open window—our seats so quiet—the motion of the cars so soothing, my friends soon gave unmistakable signs of the deep sleep that had fallen upon them;—the quiet of the night—the air so fragrant—the heavens above us so calm and starlit!

I leaned my head against the window and looked into the darkness. How calm and earnest the thoughts that came to me after the unquiet and restlessness of the day! The blessed hope of the heavenly home seemed doubly gracious. How longingly I looked upon the veil that lay between our world and the beyond! Ah! the beyond, where Christ has gone, that our life there may be perfected through him; the beyond, where many a night like this my eyes have looked upon the stars; and my soul trembled and panted, wistfully longing for more knowledge of the life above—wistfully longing for the child, the martyr child, that suffered and died upon my bosom—the child whose life on earth was so much a part of my own!—whose heavenly life I wish so much to influence my own! And I seek, I know not what, as I gaze upon those worlds above. I dare not ask for a revelation; but, ah! could I penetrate beyond the stars and catch one ray of the glorious life! Yet, the consciousness of a refined and purer existence is ever near me, as my mind separate from the earth—gives itself up to intangible and yearning inquiries, that will never be satisfied until I, too, stand within the presence of my Creator. Oh, this night time, this starlit, clear, and most pure heaven before us! Does not one see oneself more clearly, when looking upward with the ever-undefined emotion that we feel when gazing at the heavens at night?—does not our own unworthiness, our soul's need of a Saviour, come to us as our conscience, overcoming the callousness of the day and the world, whispers to us of many derelictions from our duty? of prayers hastily said over? of opportunities for good to our fellow men lost? The soft answer, the kind word and cheering smile to the world weary, all have been passed by; and we see where good, to one "of the least of these," might have made a life happier; and, as to the pure, all things are pure, so we, as we pant for the heavenly life, and the ennobling existence belonging to it, see more clearly the imperfections in this, and in our daily duties, and our need of a Mediator with him to whose pure eyes we are wholly unworthy; alas! so unworthy, that with this life our worthiness can never begin.

As we passed along nearing Vicksburg, we could see camps and camp fires, with the dim figures of men moving around them; we could see the sentinel guarding the Black River bridge, silent and erect, looking in the darkness like a dusky statue ornamenting some quaint and massive bridge of the old countries; and farther, masses of men in the road marching quietly in the night time, followed by the artillery; long lines of wagons, too, passing through the ravines—now the white covers seen on the brow of the hill; losing sight of them again, we hear the shout of the teamsters, the crack of the whip—and again catch sight of a white top through trees—and the occasional song of a wagoner. At the depot soldiers were crowded, waiting to go out; and on our arrival at our friend's, we, so weary with the excitement and turmoil of the day, were glad to rest our tired heads in calmness and peace, with no fears for the morrow, or restless forebodings of evil.

Upon reading the papers the next morning, almost the first article that caught my eye was an order from General Pemberton, insisting on all non-combatants leaving the city. "Heretofore," he said, "I have merely requested that it should be done; now I demand it." "Ah!" cried I, "have we no rest for the sole of our foot? Must we again go through the fright and anxiety of yesterday?" "We cannot leave here," replied my friend. "Where can we go? Here we are among our friends—we are welcome, and we feel in safety. Let us at least share the fate of those we love so much. If we leave, we cannot tell to what we may be exposed—even now, probably, the Federal army occupy Jackson; if we go into the country, we are liable at any time to be surrounded by them; and to whom can we apply for protection from the soldiery? We *must* stay here, even if the gentlemen say go, which, I fear, they will; we must urge them to allow us to remain, for you know they can refuse us nothing. Oh, we are so quiet and peaceful, we must stay, come what will." When the gentlemen came, we talked of the "order" with them. At first they said we must leave; but we entreated them to let us stay, representing our deplorable condition in a country overrun by soldiers, the great danger of trying to go to Mobile by railway, the track having been partly destroyed between Meridian and Jackson. We declared that we would almost starve—that we would meet any evil cheerfully in Vicksburg, where our friends were—where we were carefully housed, quiet, and contented. So, laughingly, they said they were completely overcome by our distress, and would arrange it so that we could stay if we wished. "But, remember," they said, "if trouble comes, you must meet it with your eyes open." "Yes," we said, "we can meet trouble where you are, cheerfully." All seemed to think that the matter would be decided some distance from Vicksburg, and that General Pemberton wanted to cast the responsibility from his shoulders, if the worst came, and ladies were endangered in the city.

CHAPTER VI.

RUMORS OF THE FEDERAL ADVANCE ON BLACK RIVER—GUNBOATS ON THE RIVER—CANNONADING AND FIRE AT WARRENTON—GENERAL PEMBERTON'S FORCES ENGAGED AT BLACK RIVER.

WE settled ourselves delightfully. With our sewing in the morning, and rides in the evening, our home was very pleasant—very happy and quiet. Rumors came to us of the advance of the Federal troops on Black River; yet, so uncertain were the tidings, and so slow was the advantage gained, we began to doubt almost everything. M—— was stationed below at Warrenton, and came only occasionally to see us, as the gunboats were threatening that point. Still, we were in a manner already cut off from the outer world, for the cars had ceased running farther than the Black River bridge, where General Pemberton had stationed his forces, fortifying and awaiting an attack; still, every morning the papers would tell us all was right, and our life passed on the same. Almost every day we walked up the Sky Parlor Hill, and looked through the glass at the Federal encampment near the head of the abandoned canal; we could see plainly, also, below, at a point called "Brown and Johnson's Landing," the passing of trains of wagons carrying supplies to the fleet below; we could, also, discern troops and mounted men on the opposite shore, though some miles away;—again, at the head of the canal, out in the stream, listlessly lay the dark forms of the gunboats—now two lying quite near each other—then, perhaps, a group of three, or often one alone, manned by negroes, as with the aid of the glass we could see them passing to and fro; we could see, also, the little tugboats carrying despatches from one to the other, we supposed, as frequently after their visit a transport or gunboat would put on steam and follow them up the river; we could see couriers galloping from groups of tents along the shore up to where, we presumed, the masses of the soldiers were encamped. Altogether, the Federal encampment and movements were far more stirring and interesting than the quiet fortified life of Vicksburg, waiting with calm and bristling front the result of the energetic movements beyond. We met frequently on Sky Parlor Hill an acquaintance on General Pemberton's staff, who seemed to watch with interest operations on the shore above and below us. We could see that Vicksburg was as attentively observed by the Federal troops.

The gunboats that stood out in the stream above seemed to be acting as sentinels, or on a kind of picket duty, I might call it, as a man in uniform constantly paced the deck with a large glass under his arm, which he frequently raised and took a survey of the city. But Vicksburg must have been a sealed book to him among her hills from that point of view.

One night we heard heavy cannonading an hour or two, ceasing, and then commencing again quite early in the morning, undoubtedly from the vicinity of Warrenton. How little we thought that was the commencement of music that would ring in our ears for weeks to come!—how little we thought it the beginning of trouble! That night the sky in the south was crimsoned by the light of a large fire—the cause we could not learn. The next day we heard that the little village of Warrenton had been burned by shells thrown from the boats. M—— came in that evening, and told us that the gunboats had been amusing themselves by throwing shot and shell at the fort—that very little damage had been done, except setting fire to some of the cotton composing the fort, which was still smouldering and burning slowly under the earthworks. We were told soon after by some of our friends, that the fort at Warrenton had been quietly evacuated; at least, all the guns had been taken from it and brought into Vicksburg, with ammunition, stores, &c.; the troops were left there as a blind for the time being—all this M—— did not tell me. It must have been a trial for the men to lie perfectly quiet, enduring a steady fire that they were unable to return. However, the time came when these men could look back to the shelling of Warrenton as a slight matter in comparison with the storm of shot and shell that rained upon them in the rear of Vicksburg. And now began my anxieties: M—— was below, and exposed to the firing we heard every morning and evening; and I prayed for him so fervently, feeling how utterly powerless I was, and how merciful and powerful our Father would be.

Saturday came, and with it the news that a battle was going on between the Federal troops and General Pemberton's forces at Black River; and I saw the blanching of a bright cheek, and felt, with a heavy heart, that the hopes of happiness, for many a year to come, of a dear friend, hung upon a life that would be bravely ventured there to-day. Oh! the terrible suspense of that day, when feeling that, let the result be what it would (and we trembled for it), the lives of our friends were all in all to us.

CHAPTER VII.

SUNDAY, THE 17TH—AFTER CHURCH—THE DEMORALIZED ARMY— SOLDIERS' STORIES.

SUNDAY, the 17th—the memorable seventeenth of May—as we were dressing for church, and had nearly completed the arrangement of shawls and gloves, we heard the loud booming of cannon. Frightened, for at this time we knew not *what* " an hour would bring forth," seeing no one who might account for the sudden alarm, we walked down the street, hoping to find some friend that could tell us if it were dangerous to remain away from home at church. I feared leaving my little one for any length of time, if there were any prospect of an engagement. After walking a square or two, we met an officer, who told us the report we heard proceeded from our own guns, which were firing upon a party of soldiers, who were burning some houses on the peninsula on the Louisiana shore; he told us, also, it had been rumored that General Pemberton had been repulsed

—that many citizens had gone out to attend to the wounded of yesterday's battle—all the ministers and surgeons that could leave had also gone. Still, as the bell of the Methodist church rang out clear and loud, my friend and I decided to enter, and were glad that we did so, for we heard words of cheer and comfort in this time of trouble. The speaker was a traveller, who supplied the pulpit this day, as the pastor was absent ministering to the wounded and dying on the battle field. This was a plain man, of simple, fervent words, but with so much of heart in all his exercises, that we felt, after the last hymn had been sung, the last prayer said, that we had been in a purer atmosphere. After the blessing, he requested the ladies to meet and make arrangements for lint and bandages for the wounded. As we returned home, we passed groups of anxious men at the corners, with troubled faces; very few soldiers were seen; some battery men and officers, needed for the river defences, were passing hastily up the street. Yet, in all the pleasant air and sunshine of the day, an anxious gloom seemed to hang over the faces of men: a sorrowful waiting for tidings, that all knew now, would tell of disaster. There seemed no life in the city; sullen and expectant seemed the men—tearful and hopeful the women—prayerful and hopeful, I might add; for, many a mother, groaning in spirit over the uncertainty of the welfare of those most dear to her, knelt and laid her sorrows at the foot of that Throne, where no earnest suppliant is ever rejected; where the sorrow of many a broken heart has been turned in resignation to His will who afflicts not willingly the children of men. And so, in all the dejected uncertainty, the stir of horsemen and wheels began, and wagons came rattling down the street—going rapidly one way, and then returning, seemingly, without aim or purpose: now and then a worn and dusty soldier would be seen passing with his blanket and canteen; soon, straggler after straggler came by, then groups of soldiers worn and dusty with the long march. "What can be the matter?" we all cried, as the streets and pavements became full of these worn and tired-looking men. We sent down to ask, and the reply was: "We are whipped; and the Federals are after us." We hastily seized veils and bonnets, and walked down the avenue to the iron railing that separates the yard from the street.

"Where are your going?" we asked.

No one seemed disposed to answer the question. An embarrassed, pained look came over some of the faces that were raised to us; others seemed only to feel the weariness of the long march; again we asked:

"Where on earth are you going?"

At last one man looked up in a half-surly manner, and answered:

"We are running."

"From whom?" exclaimed one of the young girls of the house.

"The Feds, to be sure," said another, half laughing and half shamefaced.

"Oh! shame on you!" cried the ladies; "and you running!"

"It's all Pem's fault," said an awkward, long-limbed, weary-looking man.

"It's all your own fault. Why don't you stand your ground?" was the reply.

"Shame on you all!" cried some of the ladies across the street, becoming excited.

I could not but feel sorry for the poor worn fellows, who did seem indeed heartily ashamed of themselves; some without arms, having probably lost them in the first break of the companies.

"We are disappointed in you!" cried some of the ladies. "Who shall we look to now for protection?"

"Oh!" said one of them, "it's the first time I ever ran. We are Georgians, and we never ran before; but we saw them all breaking and running, and we could not bear up alone."

We asked them if they did not want water; and some of them came in the yard to get it. The lady of the house offered them some supper; and while they were eating, we were so much interested, that we stood around questioning them about the result of the day. "It is all General Pemberton's fault," said a sergeant. "I'm a Missourian, and our boys stood it almost alone, not knowing what was wanted to be done; yet, fighting as long as possible, every one leaving us, and we were obliged to fall back. You know, madam, we Missourians always fight well, even if we have to retreat afterward."

"Oh!" spoke up an old man, "we would ha' fit well; but General Pemberton came up and said: 'Stand your ground, boys. Your General

Pemberton is with you;' and then, bless you, lady! the next we see'd of him, he was sitting on his horse behind a house—close, too, at that; and when we see'd that, we thought 'tain't no use, if he's going to sit there."

We could not help laughing at the old man's tale and his anger. Afterward we were told that General Pemberton behaved with courage—that the fault lay in the arrangement of troops.

And where these weary and wornout men were going, we could not tell. I think they did not know themselves.

CHAPTER VIII.

FRESH TROOPS FROM WARRENTON FOR THE INTRENCHMENTS—" WE'LL PROTECT YOU "—FEARS.

AT dark the fresh troops from Warrenton marched by, going out to the intrenchments in the rear of the city about two miles; many of the officers were fearful that the fortifications, being so incomplete, would be taken, if the Federal troops pushed immediately on, following their advantage.

As the troops from Warrenton passed by, the ladies waved their handkerchiefs, cheering them, and crying:

"These are the troops that have not run. You'll stand by us, and protect us, won't you? You won't *retreat* and bring the Federals behind you."

And the men, who were fresh and lively, swung their hats, and promised to die for the ladies—never to run—never to retreat; while the poor fellows on the pavement, sitting on their blankets—lying on the ground—leaning against trees, or anything to rest their wearied bodies, looked on silent and dejected. They were not to blame, these poor, weary fellows. If they were unsuccessful, it is what many a man has been before them; and then, endurance of the long fasts in the rifle pits, and coolness amid the showers of ball and shell thrown at devoted Vicksburg afterward, show us that men, though unfortunate, can retrieve their character.

"There has been many a life lost to-day," said a soldier to me—"many an officer and man."

"Ah! truly, yes," I said; for the ambulances had been passing with wounded and dead; and one came slowly by with officers riding near it, bearing the dead body of General Tilghman, the blood dripping slowly from it. We were told, also, of a friend who had been mortally wounded.

What a sad evening we spent—continually hearing of friends and acquaintances left dead on the field, or mortally wounded, and being brought in ambulances to the hospital! We almost feared to retire that night; no one seemed to know whether the Federal army was advancing or not; some told us that they were many miles away, and others that they were quite near. How did we know but in the night we might be awakened by the tumult of their arrival!

The streets were becoming quiet; the noise and bustle had died out with the excitement of the day, and, save now and then the rapid passing of some officer, or army wagon, they were almost deserted. And what will the morrow bring forth? I thought, as I leaned from the balcony of my room; will these streets echo to the tread of the victorious army? I shrank from the thought. Without protectors, what might be our fate?—to be turned from our homes, perhaps, widows and orphans. But the heavens above so calm—so smooth and soothing—the quiet glide of the silent river—and the wind swaying the trees with a monotonous wave—quelled and laid these thoughts of evil; and the blessed trust and faith in Him who is all powerful came with renewed balm to my anxious heart.

CHAPTER IX.

THE BALL IN MOTION—VIEW FROM THE COURT HOUSE—FEDERAL PRISONERS SENT ACROSS THE RIVER—MOVEMENTS OF GUNBOAT.

THE next morning all was quiet; we heard no startling rumors; the soldiers were being gathered together and taken out into the rifle pits; Vicksburg was regularly besieged, and we were to stay at our homes and watch the progress of the battle. The rifle pits and intrenchments were almost two miles from the city. We would be out of danger, so we thought; but we did not know what was in preparation for us around the bend of the river. The day wore on; still all was quiet. At night our hopes revived: the Federal troops had not yet come up—another calm night and morning. At three o'clock that evening, the artillery boomed from the intrenchments, roar after roar, followed by the rattle of musketry: the Federal forces were making their first attack. Looking out from the back veranda, we could plainly see the smoke before the report of the guns reached us. Our anxiety was great, indeed, having been told by gentlemen the night before, that the works in the rear of Vicksburg were anything but of a superior kind.

The discharges of musketry were irregular. Yet, to us who were thinking of the dear ones exposed to this frequent firing, the restless forebodings and unhappiness caused by the distant din of battle pained us indeed. After listening for some time to the reports, which sounded to us, in the distance, like the quick, successive droppings of balls on sheet iron, again and again sounded the cannon like thunderings near us. At every report our hearts beat quicker. The excitement was intense in the city. Groups of people stood on every available position where a view could be obtained of the distant hills, where the jets of white smoke constantly passed out from among the trees.

Some of our friends proposed going for a better view up on the balcony around the cupola of the court house. The view from there was most extensive and beautiful. Hill after hill arose in the distance, enclosing the city in the form of a crescent. Immediately in the centre and east of the river, the firing seemed more continuous, while to the left and running northly, the rattle and roar would be sudden, sharp, and vigorous, then ceasing for some time. The hills around near the city, and indeed every place that seemed commanding and secure, was covered with anxious spectators—many of them ladies—fearing the result of the afternoon's conflict. To the extreme left and north, near the river, the warfare became general, while toward the centre the firing became less rapid.

What a beautiful landscape lay out before us! Far in the distance lay the cultivated hills—some already yellow with grain, while on other hills and in the valleys the deep green of the trees formed the shadows in the fair landscape.

It was amid the clump of trees on the far distant hillside, that the Federal batteries could be discerned by the frequent puffings of smoke from the guns. Turning to the river, we could see a gunboat that had the temerity to come down as near the town as possible, and lay just out of reach of the Confederate batteries, with steam up.

Two more lay about half a mile above and

nearer the canal; two or three transports had gotten up steam, and lay near the mouth of the canal. Below the city a gunboat had come up and landed, out of reach, on the Louisiana side, striving to engage the lower batteries of the town —firing about every fifteen minutes. While we were looking at the river, we saw two large yawls start out from shore, with two larger boats tied to them, and full of men.

We learned that they were the Federal prisoners that had been held in the town, and to-day paroled and sent over to the Federal encampment, so that the resources of the garrison might be husbanded as much as possible, and the necessity of sustaining them avoided.

The idea made me serious. We might look forward truly now to perhaps real suffering.

Yet, I did not regret my resolution to remain, and would have left the town more relunctantly to-day than ever before, for we felt that now, indeed, the whole country was unsafe, and that our only hope of safety lay in Vicksburg.

The little boats, with their prisoners, had gained the opposite shore; and we could see the liberated men walking along the river bank; we could see, also, the little steamtug coming down, and stopping at the gunboat near the city; it, also, visited the transports and the gunboats near the canal, and then, leaving, steamed with much swiftness up the river toward the mouth of the Yazoo.

In looking again with a glass in the rear of the city, we could see the Southern soldiers working at their guns, and walking in the rear of a fort on a hill nearer by. The Federal troops were too distant to discern.

Some ambulances were coming into the city, probably bringing the wounded from the field.

We saw an officer coming in with his head bound up and his arm in a sling, his servant walking by his side leading his horse. Aside from the earnest group of spectators moving from one place to another, the town seemed perfectly quiet.

Looking again toward the river, the gunboat near the lower batteries kept its old position, slowly firing at the lower part of the city; and far over on the other shore, walking rapidly, I observed the figures of the freed prisoners near the canal, and fast becoming indistinct, even with the aid of a glass.

So twilight began falling over the scene—hushing to an occasional report the noise and uproar of the battle field—falling softly and silently upon the river—separating us more and more from the raging passions surging around us—bringing only the heaven above us, and the small space of life we occupy, distinctly to our eyes.

CHAPTER X.

GROUNDLESS FEAR OF AN ATTACK BY GUNBOATS—SHELLS FALL—THE BOMBARDMENT BEGINS—CAVE SHELTER—GARRISON FORCE—CAVES AND CAVE LIFE.

FROM gentlemen who called on the evening of the attack in the rear of the town, we learned that it was quite likely, judging from the movements on the river, that the gunboats would make an attack that night. We remained dressed during the night; once or twice we sprang to our feet, startled by the report of a cannon; but after waiting in the darkness of the veranda for some time, the perfect quiet of the city convinced us that our alarm was needless.

Next day, two or three shells were thrown from the battle field, exploding near the house. This was our first shock, and a severe one. We did not dare to go in the back part of the house all day.

Some of the servants came and got down by us for protection, while others kept on with their work as if feeling a perfect contempt for the shells.

In the evening we were terrified and much excited by the loud rush and scream of mortar shells; we ran to the small cave near the house, and were in it during the night, by this time wearied and almost stupefied by the loss of sleep.

The caves were plainly becoming a necessity, as some persons had been killed on the street by fragments of shells. The room that I had so lately slept in had been struck by a fragment of a shell during the first night, and a large hole made in the ceiling. I shall never forget my extreme fear during the night, and my utter hopelessness of ever seeing the morning light. Terror stricken, we remained crouched in the cave, while shell after shell followed each other in quick succession. I endeavored by constant prayer to prepare myself for the sudden death I was almost certain awaited me. My heart stood still as we would hear the reports from the guns, and the rushing and fearful sound of the shell as it came toward us. As it neared, the noise became more deafening; the air was full of the rushing sound; pains darted through my temples; my ears were full of the confusing noise; and, as it exploded, the report flashed through my head like an electric shock, leaving me in a quiet state of terror the most painful that I can imagine—cowering in a corner, holding my child to my heart—the only feeling of my life being the choking throbs of my heart, that rendered me almost breathless. As singly they fell short, or beyond the cave, I was aroused by a feeling of thankfulness that was of short duration. Again and again the terrible fright came over us in that night.

I saw one fall in the road without the mouth of the cave, like a flame of fire, making the earth tremble, and, with a low, singing sound, the fragments sped on in their work of death.

Morning found us more dead than alive, with blanched faces and trembling lips. We were not reassured on hearing, from a man who took refuge in the cave, that a mortar shell in falling would not consider the thickness of earth above us a circumstance.

Some of the ladies, more courageous by daylight, asked him what he was in there for, if that was the case. He was silenced for an hour, when he left. As the day wore on, and we were still preserved, though the shells came as ever, we were somewhat encouraged.

3*

The next morning we heard that Vicksburg would not in all probability hold out more than a week or two, as the garrison was poorly provisioned; and one of General Pemberton's staff officers told us that the effective force of the garrison, upon being estimated, was found to be fifteen thousand men; General Loring having been cut off after the battle of Black River, with probably ten thousand.

The ladies all cried, "Oh, never surrender!" but after the experience of the night, I really could not tell what I wanted, or what my opinions were.

How often I thought of M—— upon the battle field, and his anxiety for us in the midst of this unanticipated danger, wherein the safety lay entirely on the side of the belligerent gentlemen, who were shelling us so furiously, at least two miles from the city, in the bend of the river near the canal.

So constantly dropped the shells around the city, that the inhabitants all made preparations to live under the ground during the siege. M—— sent over and had a cave made in a hill near by. We seized the opportunity one evening, when the

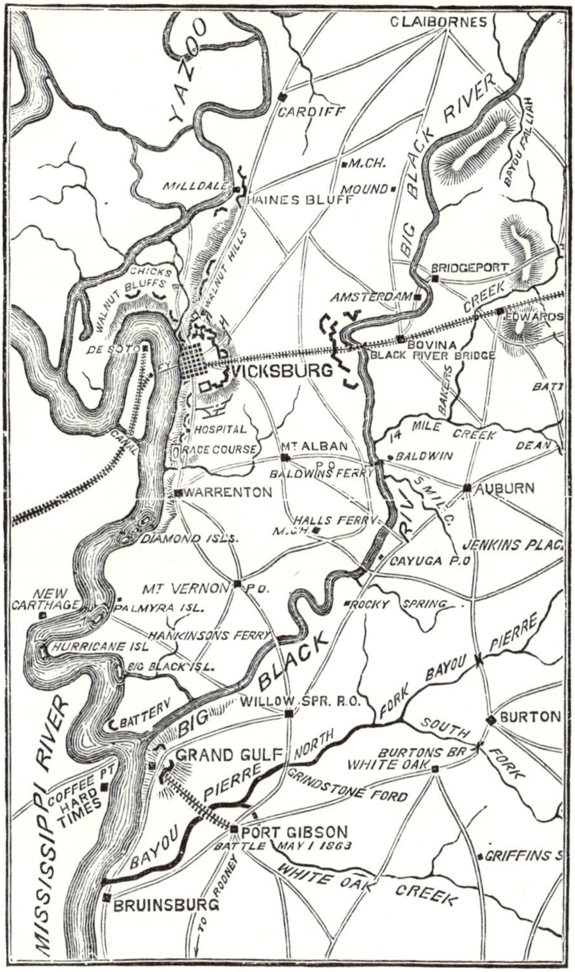
CLAIBORNES
YAZOO
CARDIFF
M.CH.
MILLDALE
MOUND
HAINES BLUFF
BIG BLACK RIVER
BAYOU FALLIAH
WALNUT HILLS
CHICKS
WALNUT BLUFFS
BRIDGEPORT
AMSTERDAM
CREEK
EDWARDS
DE SOTO
BOVINA
BLACK RIVER BRIDGE
VICKSBURG
BAKERS
CANAL
HOSPITAL
RACE COURSE
MT ALBAN
P.O.
14 MILE CREEK
BALDWIN
DEAN
BALDWINS FERRY
WARRENTON
AUBURN
HALLS FERRY
M.CH.
DIAMOND ISLS.
JENKINS PLAC
CAYUGA P.O
MT VERNON P.O.
NEW CARTHAGE
PALMYRA ISL.
ROCKY SPRING
HANKINSONS FERRY
HURRICANE ISL
BIG BLACK ISL.
BIG BLACK
BAYOU PIERRE
WILLOW SPR. P.O.
FORK
BATTERY
BURTON
SOUTH
GRAND GULF
NORTH
BURTONS BR
WHITE OAK
MISSISSIPPI RIVER
COFFEE PT
HARD TIMES
GRINDSTONE FORD
FORK
PIERRE
PORT GIBSON
BATTLE MAY 1 1863
BAYOU
GRIFFINS
WHITE OAK CREEK
BRUINSBURG
TO RODNEY

gunners were probably at their supper, for we had a few moments of quiet, to go over and take possession. We were under the care of a friend of M——, who was paymaster on the staff of the same General with whom M—— was Adjutant. We had neighbors on both sides of us; and it would have been an amusing sight to a spectator to witness the domestic scenes presented without by the number of servants preparing the meals under the high bank containing the caves.

Our dining, breakfasting, and supper hours were quite irregular. When the shells were falling fast, the servants came in for safety, and our meals waited for completion some little time; again they would fall slowly, with the lapse of many minutes between, and out would start the cooks to their work.

Some families had light bread made in large quantities, and subsisted on it with milk (provided their cows were not killed from one milking time to another), without any more cooking, until called on to replenish. Though most of us lived on corn bread and bacon, served three times a day, the only luxury of the meal consisting in its warmth, I had some flour, and frequently had some hard, tough biscuit made from it, there being no soda or yeast to be procured. At this time we could, also, procure beef. A gentleman friend was kind enough to offer me his camp bed, a narrow spring mattress, which fitted within the contracted cave very comfortably; another had his tent fly stretched over the mouth of our residence to shield us from the sun; and thus I was the recipient of many favors, and under obligations to many gentlemen of the army for delicate and kind attentions; and, in looking back to my trials at that time, I shall ever remember with gratitude the kindness with which they strove to ward off every deprivation. And so I went regularly to work, keeping house under ground. Our new habitation was an excavation made in the earth, and branching six feet from the entrance, forming a cave in the shape of a T. In one of the wings my bed fitted; the other I used as a kind of a dressing room; in this the earth had been cut down a foot or two below the floor of the main cave; I could stand erect here; and when tired of sitting in other portions of my residence, I bowed myself into it, and stood impassively resting at full height—one of the variations in the still shell-expectant life. M——'s servant cooked for us under protection of the hill. Our quarters were close, indeed; yet I was more comfortable than I expected I could have been made under the earth in that fashion.

We were safe at least from fragments of shell —and they were flying in all directions; though no one seemed to think our cave any protection, should a mortar shell happen to fall directly on top of the ground above us. We had our roof arched and braced, the supports of the bracing taking up much room in our confined quarters. The earth was about five feet thick above, and seemed hard and compact; yet, poor M——, every time he came in, examined it, fearing, amid some of the shocks it sustained, that it might crack and fall upon us.

CHAPTER XI.

BURIED ALIVE—HOUSE BREAKING—APPEARANCE OF SHELL AT NIGHT—UNDER THE ROOT OF A FIG TREE.

ONE afternoon, amid the rush and explosion of the shells, cries and screams arose—the screams of women amid the shrieks of the falling shells. The servant boy, George, after starting and coming back once or twice, his timidity overcoming his curiosity (I was not at all surprised at it), at last gathered courage to go to the ravine near us, from whence the cries proceeded, and found that a negro man had been buried alive within a cave, he being alone at that time. Workmen were instantly set to deliver him, if possible; but when found, the unfortunate man had evidently been dead some little time. His wife and relations were distressed beyond measure, and filled the air with their cries and groans.

This incident made me doubly doubtful of my cave; I feared that I might be buried alive at any time. Another incident happened the same day: A gentleman, resident of Vicksburg, had a large cave made, and repeatedly urged his wife to leave the house and go into it. She steadily refused, and, being quite an invalid, was lying on the bed, when he took her by the hand and insisted upon her accompanying him so strongly, that she yielded; and they had scarcely left the house, when a mortar shell went crashing through, utterly demolishing the bed that had so lately been vacated, tearing up the floor, and almost completely destroying the room.

That night, after my little one had been laid in bed, I sat at the mouth of the cave, with the servants drawn around me, watching the brilliant display of fireworks the mortar boats were making—the passage of the shell, as it travelled through the heavens, looking like a swiftly moving star. As it fell, it approached the earth so rapidly, that it seemed to leave behind a track of fire.

This night we kept our seats, as they all passed rapidly over us, none falling near. The incendiary shells were still more beautiful in appearance. As they exploded in the air, the burning matter and balls fell like large, clear blue-and-amber stars, scattering hither and thither.

"Miss M——," said one of the more timid servants, "do they want to kill us all dead? Will they keep doing this until we all die?"

I said most heartily, "I hope not."

The servants we had with us seemed to possess more courage than is usually attributed to negroes. They seldom hesitated to cross the street for water at any time. The "boy" slept at the entrance of the cave, with a pistol I had given him, telling me I need not be " afeared—dat any one dat come dar would have to go over his body first."

He never refused to carry out any little article to M—— on the battle field. I laughed heartily at a dilemma he was placed in one day: The mule that he had mounted to ride out to the battle field took him to a dangerous locality, where the shells were flying thickly, and then, suddenly stopping, through fright, obstinately refused to stir. It was in vain that George kicked and beat him—go he would not; so, clenching his hand, he hit him severely in the head several times, jumped down, ran home, and left him. The mule stood a few minutes rigidly, then, looking round, and seeing George at some distance from him, turned and followed, quite demurely.

Each day, as the couriers came into the city, M—— would write me little notes, asking after our welfare, and telling me of the progress of the siege. I, in return, would write to him of our safety, but was always careful in speaking of the danger to which we were exposed. I thought poor M—— had enough to try him, without suffering anxiety for us; so I made light of my fears, which were in reality wearing off rapidly. Every week he came in to make inquiries in person. In his letters he charged me particularly to be careful of the provisions—that no one could tell what our necessities might be.

In one of his letters, he says: "Already I am living on pea meal, and cannot think of your coming to this." One thing I had learned quite lately in my cave was to make good bread: one of my cave neighbors had given me yeast and instructions. I, in turn, had instructed a servant, so that when we used the flour it could be presented in a more inviting form

One morning, after breakfast, the shells began falling so thickly around us, that they seemed aimed at the particular spot on which our cave was located. Two or three fell immediately in the rear of it, exploding a few moments before reaching the ground, and the fragments went singing over the top of our habitation. I, at length, became so much alarmed—as the cave trembled excessively—for our safety, that I determined, rather than be buried alive, to stand out from under the earth; so, taking my child in my arms, and calling the servants, we ran to a refuge near the roots of a large fig tree, that branched out over the bank, and served as a protection from the fragments of shells. As we stood trembling there—for the shells were falling all around us—some of my gentlemen friends came up to reassure me, telling me that the tree would protect us, and that the range would probably be changed in a short time. While they spoke, a shell, that seemed to be of enormous size, fell, screaming and hissing, immediately before the mouth of our cave, within a few feet of the entrance, sending up a huge column of smoke and earth, and jarring the ground most sensibly where we stood. What seemed very strange, the earth closed in around the shell, and left only the newly upturned soil to show where it had fallen.

Long it was before the range was changed, and

the frightful missiles fell beyond us—long before I could resolve to return to our sadly threatened home.

I found on my return that the walls were seamed here and there with cracks, but the earth had remained firm above us. I took possession again, with resignation, yet in fear and trembling.

CHAPTER XII.

FIRE AT NIGHT—A NARROW ESCAPE—MOONLIGHT—SHELLS FROM THE BATTLE FIELD—EMPLOYMENT AND TRAFFIC.

MY past resolution having forsaken me, again were the mortar shells heard with extreme terror, and I was many days recovering the equanimity I had been so long attaining. This night, as a few nights before, a large fire raged in the town. I was told that a large storehouse, filled with commissary stores, was burning, casting lurid lights over the devoted city; and amid all, fell—with screams and violent explosions, flinging the fatal fragments in all directions—our old and relentless enemies, the mortar shells.

The night was so warm, and the cave so close, that I tried to sit out at the entrance, George saying he would keep watch and tell when they were falling toward us. Soon the report of the gun would be heard, and George, standing on the hillock of loose earth, near the cave, looked intently upward; while I, with suspended breath, would listen anxiously as he cried, "Here she comes! going over!" then again, "Coming—falling—falling right dis way!" Then I would spring to my feet, and for a moment hesitate about the protection of the cave. Suddenly, as the rushing descent was heard, I would beat a precipitate retreat into it, followed by the servants.

That night I could scarcely sleep, the explosions were so loud and frequent. Before we retired, George had been lying without the door. I had arisen about twelve o'clock, and stood looking out at the different courses of light marking the passage of the shells, when I noticed that George was not in his usual place at the entrance. On looking out, I saw that he was sleeping soundly, some little distance off, and many fragments of shell falling near him. I aroused him, telling him to come to the entrance for safety. He had scarcely started, when a huge piece of shell came whizzing along, which fortunately George dodged in time, and it fell in the very spot where he had so lately slept.

Fearing to retire, I sat in the moonlight at the entrance, the square of light that lay in the doorway causing our little bed, with the sleeping child, to be set out in relief against the dark wall of the cave—causing the little mirror and a picture or two I had hung against the wall to show misshapen lengths of shadows—tinting the crimson shawl that draped the entrance of my little dressing room, with light on the outer folds, and darkening in shadow the inner curves;—beautifying all, this silvery glow of moonlight, within the darkened earth—beautifying my heart with lighter and more hopeful thoughts. Whatever the sins of the world may have brought us to—however dark and fearful the life to which man may subject us, our Heavenly Father ever blesseth us alike with the sun's warmth and the moon's beauty—ever blesseth us with the hope that, when our toil and travail here are ended, the peace and the beautiful life of heaven will be ours.

Days wore on, and the mortar shells had passed over continually without falling near us; so that I became quite at my ease, in view of our danger, when one of the Federal batteries opposite the intrenchments altered their range; so that, at about six o'clock every evening, Parrott shells came whirring into the city, frightening the inhabitants of caves wofully.

Our policy in building had been to face directly away from the river, and all caves were prepared, as near as possible, in this manner. As the fragments of shells continued with the same impetus after the explosion, in but one direction, onward, they were not likely to reach us, fronting in this manner with their course.

But this was unexpected—guns throwing shells from the battle field directly at the entrance of our caves. Really, was there to be no mental rest for the women of Vicksburg?

The cave we inhabited was about five squares from the levee. A great many had been made in a hill immediately beyond us; and near this hill we could see most of the shells fall. Caves were the fashion—the rage—over besieged Vicksburg. Negroes, who understood their business, hired themselves out to dig them, at from thirty to fifty dollars, according to the size. Many persons, considering different localities unsafe, would sell them to others, who had been less fortunate, or less provident; and so great was the demand for cave workmen, that a new branch of industry sprang up and became popular—particularly as the personal safety of the workmen was secured, and money withal.

CHAPTER XIII.

SHELLS FROM THE REAR OF THE CITY—PROVIDENTIAL DELIVERANCE —PANTOMIME—PEA MEAL—HOSPITAL ACCIDENT.

It was about four o'clock, one Wednesday evening—the shelling during the day had gone on about as usual—I was reading in safety, I imagined, when the unmistakable whirring of Parrott shells told us that the battery we so much feared had opened from the intrenchments. I ran to the entrance to call the servants in; and immediately after they entered, a shell struck the earth a few feet from the entrance, burying itself without exploding. I ran to the little dressing room, and could hear them striking around us on all sides. I crouched closely against the wall, for I did not know at what moment one might strike within the cave. A man came in much frightened, and asked to remain until the danger was over. The servants stood in the little niche by the bed, and the man took refuge in the small ell where I was stationed. He had been there but a short time, standing in front of me, and near the wall, when a Parrott shell came whirling in at the entrance, and fell in the centre of the cave before us all, lying there smoking. Our eyes were fastened upon it, while we expected every moment the terrific explosion would ensue. I pressed my child closer to my heart, and drew nearer to the wall. Our fate seemed almost certain. The poor man who had sought refuge within was most exposed of all. With a sudden impulse, I seized a large double blanket that lay near, and gave it to him for the purpose of shielding him from the fragments; and thus we remained for a moment, with our eyes fixed in terror on the missile of death, when George, the servant boy, rushed forward, seized the shell, and threw it into the street, running swiftly in the opposite direction. Fortunately, the fuse had become nearly extinguished, and the shell fell harmless—remaining near the mouth of the cave, as a trophy of the fearlessness of the servant and our remarkable escape. Very thankful was I for our preservation, which was the theme of conversation for a day among our cave neighbors. The incident of the blanket was also related; and all laughed heartily at my wise supposition that the blanket could be any protection from the heavy fragments of shells.

Nor was this all: I had occasion to go to the mouth of the cave one evening to speak to George; and there, with an enlightened audience of servants from the surrounding caves collected near him, George was going through a grave pantomime of the whole affair. It seems that he expected the refugee to act the part of preserver in our extremity, and throw out the shell; but, as he was disappointed in the matter, he represented him in the most ridiculous manner possible to the audience.

Pressing up closely to the wheel of a wagon near by, George extended his eyes, holding out his hand as if with a shield, and shrinking with the semblance of extreme terror, that amused his spectators vastly: then, changing the whole character, he put on the bravest port imaginable, pushing his hat, with an independent air, on the side of his head; and, assuming a don't-carish look, he sauntered forward to a large piece of shell that lay conveniently near, caught it with both hands, gave it a careless swing and throw far different from the reality, turned on his heels, walked back to the wagon, with the peculiar swinging step of a proud negro; then, leaning his arm on the wheel, carelessly surveyed his audience, with a look that plainly said, " What you think o' dat, niggars?" The benefited group immediately began laughing and applauding, like a well-trained bevy of *claqueurs*, in which they were soon joined by George himself.

Soon after, I received a note from M——, imploring me to be careful and remain within the cave constantly. I could see that he was restless and troubled in regard to the new peril from the battle field.

And so the weary days went on—the long, weary days—when we could not tell in what terrible form death might come to us before the sun went down. Another fear that troubled M—— was, that our provisions might not last us during the siege. He would frequently urge me to husband all that I had, for troublesome times were probably in store for us; told me of the soldiers in the intrenchments, who would have gladly eaten the bread that was left from our meals, for they were suffering every privation, and that our servants lived far better than these men who were defending the city. Soon the pea meal became an article of food for us also, and a very unpalatable article it proved. To make it of proper consistency, we were obliged to mix some corn meal with it, which cooked so much faster than the pea meal, that it burned before the bread was half done. The taste was peculiar and disagreeable.

However, it soon proved unwholesome, for the soldiers were again allowed to draw rations of the remaining corn meal, with the peas in the kernel to be boiled with meat. We were, indeed, experiencing the rigors and hardships of a siege, for we ate nothing now but meat and bread.

Still, we had nothing to complain of in comparison with the soldiers: many of them were sick and wounded in a hospital in the most exposed parts of the city, with shells falling and exploding all around them. One shell went completely through a hospital in the centre of the city, without exploding or injuring any one, save by the severe shock to the invalids: a fragment afterward came through the side of the same house, severely fracturing the hip of a soldier, who was lying already wounded; one or two wounded men were, also, killed by fragments of shell while in the hospital.

CHAPTER XIV.

DOGS—HORSES—DESCENT OF A SHELL THROUGH A CAVE—A MOTHER'S CRIES—DESERTED HOMES—SILENCE.

EVEN the very animals seemed to share the general fear of a sudden and frightful death. The dogs would be seen in the midst of the noise to gallop up the street, and then to return, as if fear had maddened them. On hearing the descent of a shell, they would dart aside—then, as it exploded, sit down and howl in the most pitiful manner. There were many walking the street, apparently without homes. George carried on a continual warfare with them, as they came about the fire where our meals were cooking.

In the midst of other miserable thoughts, it came into my mind one day, that these dogs through hunger might become as much to be dreaded as wolves. Groundless was this anxiety, for in the course of a week or two they had almost disappeared.

The horses, belonging to the officers, and fastened to the trees near the tents, would frequently strain the halter to its full length, rearing high in the air, with a loud snort of terror, as a shell would explode near. I could hear them in the night cry out in the midst of the uproar, ending in a low, plaintive whinny of fear.

The poor creatures subsisted entirely on cane tops and mulberry leaves. Many of the mules and horses had been driven outside of the lines, by order of General Pemberton, for subsistence. Only mules enough were left, belonging to the Confederacy, to allow three full teams to a regiment. Private property was not interfered with.

Sitting in the cave, one evening, I heard the most heartrending screams and moans. I was told that a mother had taken a child into a cave about a hundred yards from us; and having laid it on its little bed, as the poor woman believed, in safety, she took her seat near the entrance of the cave. A mortar shell came rushing through the air, and fell with much force, entering the earth above the sleeping child—cutting through into the cave—oh! most horrible sight to the mother—crushing in the upper part of the little sleeping head, and taking away the young innocent life without a look or word of passing love to be treasured in the mother's heart.

I sat near the square of moonlight, silent and sorrowful, hearing the sobs and cries—hearing the moans of a mother for her dead child—the child that a few moments since lived to caress and love —speaking the tender words that endear so much the tie of mother and child. Oh, the little lonely grave! so far distant, yet so ever present with me; the sunny, auburn head that I laid there six months after this terrible war began!

I could not hear those sobs and cries without thinking of the night—that last night—when I held my darling to my heart, thinking that, though so suddenly stricken and so scared, she would still live to bless my life. And the terrible awakening!—to find that, lying in my arms all my own, as I believed, she was going swiftly— going into the far unknown eternity! Sliding from my embrace, the precious life was called by One so mighty—so all-powerful—yet so merciful, that I bowed my head in silence.

Still the moans from the bereaved mother came borne on the pleasant air, floating through the silvery moonlit scene—saddening hearts that had never known sorrow, and awakening chords of sympathy in hearts that before had thrilled and suffered. Yet, " it is better to have loved and lost than never to have loved at all." Yes, better the tender memory of a hidden life that glows in our hearts forever; better, all will say who have known the light and consolation given from on high, when we throw ourselves before His Throne in utter wretchedness, and arise strong—strong in the strength that never faileth—the Lord's strength. The desert that hath not known the oases of life, though blasted and withered by the burning sirocco that passeth over, cannot know the refreshing and gentle drops that bring renewed and more tender verdure.

How very sad this life in Vicksburg!—how little security can we feel, with so many around us seeing the morning light that will never more see the night! I could not sit quietly within hearing of so much grief; and, leaving my seat, I paced backward and forward before the low entrance of my house. The court-house bell tolled twelve; and though the shells fell slowly still around the spot where the young life had gone out, yet friends were going to and from the place.

How blightingly the hand of warfare lay upon the town! even in the softening light of the moon—the closed and desolate houses—the gardens, with gates half open, and cattle standing amid the loveliest flowers and verdure! This carelessness of appearance and evident haste of departure was visible everywhere—the inhabitants, in this perilous time, feeling only anxiety for personal safety and the strength of their cave homes.

The moans of pain came slowly and more indistinct, until all was silent; and the bereaved mother slept, I hope—slept to find, on waking, a dull pressure of pain at her heart, and in the first collection of faculties will wonder what it is. Then her care for the child will return, and the new sorrow will again come to her—gone, forever gone!

It will take days to fully realize it, and then she will struggle and grow strong. God in his mercy helps the poor human hearts that suffer, struggle, and grow strong in these sad years of warfare! No one came now—no word to show that life still throbbed in the silent city.

The fresh air told of the coming morning: the guns were still. Peace for a short time reigned in the troubled city; and, in the perfect quiet that prevailed, my eyes grew heavy, and I once more sought my bed—this time to rest peacefully until the cheerful morning light dawned upon us.

CHAPTER XV.

AN EXCITEMENT—SINKING OF THE CINCINNATI—SKY PARLOR HILL—
MOVING PROSPECTS.

WITH the dawn came the old unrest and distrust, for the shells were again falling quite thickly around us; and I passed an hour or two in continual shrinkings and exclamations. At length our tormentors passed farther on, and I again felt relieved from anxiety.

At ten or twelve o'clock, we saw, in spite of the continual falling of the shells, gentlemen hurrying toward the river. Soon we heard the Confederate river batteries booming loudly, and then all was silent. What could it mean? I did not venture to look without; and so I sat waiting for some one to come to me. At last a friend appeared, who, in the most triumphant manner, told us that the Confederates had routed the Federal fleet. The gunboats had formed in line of battle, sailing down majestically, with the Cincin-

nati—one of the finest boats in the river navy—
leading the attack.

She came rapidly down around the point of
the peninsula—the signal guns silent—when the
battery, containing the Brooks gun, opened on
her, as she came within range. The first shot cut
down the flag; the second struck her side; and
the third, the Brooks ball, with the steel wedge,
cut into the iron plates near the water's edge.
She turned immediately, and steamed back up
the river in a sinking condition. The remaining
boats, also, changed their course and retired. The
Cincinnati had scarcely turned the point, when
she sank near the shore.

"Ah! yes!" said the Major, "had it not
been for the fortunate sinking of the Cincinnati,
you would have become conscious of a fearful
warfare raging in the city. Had the boats gotten
opposite and engaged our batteries, the firing
would have been terrific."

The Major also told us that many ladies had
been so much interested in the expected engagement, that they had gone up on Sky Parlor Hill
for a better view.

It has been said that the Federal guns have

never been sufficiently elevated to throw shell and shot so high as Sky Parlor Hill; yet, I should not like to risk my life for mere curiosity sake, when it was not possible to be of any service.

The Sky Parlor Hill is so called from its extreme height, being a portion of the bluff that stood where the principal commercial street now stands, the grading of the city having taken most of the elevation down. The hill now occupies about a square—the distance of two squares from the river—and is a prominent feature from all parts of the city. A rugged drive winds on one side up the steep ascent, and a long and dizzy flight of wooden steps ascend from the street on the opposite side.

It is surmounted by a little house that one could imagine surmounted "the bean stalk," in the celebrated history of "Jack," quaint and old, yet one that the earlier inhabitants would have called a "fine house."

The view—and that is what the place is visited for—is good, both of the city and river, for some miles above. Crowds of people collect here on the occasion of any move being made in the direction of the river.

A large trunk was picked up after the sinking of the Cincinnati, belonging to a surgeon on board. It contained valuable surgical instruments that could not be procured in the Confederacy; a letter, also, written to the gentleman's wife previous to the departure of the fleet from above, telling her that the letter would be mailed at Vicksburg, as there was no doubt whatever that the place would be taken when an attack was made from the river.

It was also said that Commodore Porter was aboard the Cincinnati. How the fact was ascertained, no one could tell.

Shortly after the sinking of the Cincinnati, I received a note from M——, saying that he was very much troubled in regard to our safety in the city—fearing that some time a mortar shell might fall on our cave, or that the constant jarring of the earth from the near explosion might cause it to seam and fall upon us. Therefore, he had decided to have a home made for me near the battle field, where he was stationed—one that would be entirely out of reach of the mortar shells. I was positively shocked at the idea—going to the battle field ! where ball and shell fell without intermission. Was M—— in earnest? I could scarcely believe it.

A friend came soon after, and told me that I would find my home on the battle field far more pleasant and safe than the one in town—that we were protected from the fragments only in our cave—that on the battle field the missiles were of far less weight, and in falling far less dangerous.

We were to experience our last and nearest explosion of the never-to-be-forgotten mortar shells before we left. M—— had written to me to be ready on the following night. As the moon was not shining, the firing from the Federal batteries would cease at dark; afterward we could go out without interruption. I was delighted at the prospect of a change in our mouldy lives, and looked forward to our ride—after dark though it was—with the utmost pleasure.

CHAPTER XVI.

FALL OF A SHELL AT THE CORNER OF MY CAVE—MUSIC—CASUALTIES OF THE DAY.

I was sitting near the entrance, about five o'clock, thinking of the pleasant change—oh, bless me!—that to-morrow would bring, when the bombardment commenced more furiously than usual, the shells falling thickly around us, causing vast columns of earth to fly upward, mingled with smoke. As usual, I was uncertain whether to remain within or run out. As the rocking and trembling of the earth was very distinctly felt, and the explosions alarmingly near, I stood within the mouth of the cave ready to make my escape, should one chance to fall above our domicile. In my anxiety I was startled by the shouts of the servants and a most fearful jar and rocking of the earth, followed by a deafening explosion, such as I had never heard before. The cave filled instantly with powder smoke and dust. I stood with a tingling, prickling sensation in my head, hands, and feet, and with a confused brain. Yet alive!—was the first glad thought that came to me;—child, servants, all here, and saved!—from some great danger, I felt. I stepped out, to find a group of persons before my cave, looking anxiously for me; and lying all around, freshly torn, rose bushes, arbor-vitæ trees, large clods of earth, splinters, pieces of plank, wood, &c. A mortar shell had struck the corner of the cave, fortunately so near the brow of the hill, that it had gone obliquely into the earth, exploding as it went, breaking large masses from the side of the hill—tearing away the fence, the shrubbery and flowers — sweeping all, like an avalanche, down near the entrance of my good refuge.

I stood dismayed, and surveyed the havoc that had been made around me, while our little family under it all had been mercifully preserved. Though many of the neighboring servants had been standing near at the time, not one had been injured in the slightest degree; yet, pieces of plank, fragments of earth, and splinters had fallen in all directions. A portion of earth from the roof of my cave had been dislodged and fallen. Saving this, it remained intact.

That evening some friends sat with me : one took up my guitar and played some pretty little airs for us; yet, the noise of the shells threw a discord among the harmonies. To me it seemed like the crushing and bitter spirit of hate near the light and grace of happiness. How could we sing and laugh amid our suffering fellow beings—amid the shriek of death itself?

This, only breaking the daily monotony of our lives!—this thrilling knowledge of sudden and horrible death occurring near us, told to-night and forgotten in to-morrow's renewal!—this sad news of a Vicksburg day! A little negro child, playing in the yard, had found a shell; in rolling and turning it, had innocently pounded the fuse; the terrible explosion followed, showing, as the white cloud of smoke floated away, the mangled remains of a life that to the mother's heart had possessed all of beauty and joy.

A young girl, becoming weary in the confinement of the cave, hastily ran to the house in the interval that elapsed between the slowly falling shells. On returning, an explosion sounded near her—one wild scream, and she ran into her mother's presence, sinking like a wounded dove, the life blood flowing over the light summer dress in crimson ripples from a death-wound in her side, caused by the shell fragment.

A fragment had also struck and broken the arm of a little boy playing near the mouth of his mother's cave. This was one day's account.

I told of my little girl's great distress when the shells fell thickly near us—how she ran to me breathless, hiding her head in my dress without a word; then cautiously looking out, with her anxious face questioning, would say: "Oh! mamma, was it a mortar tell?" Poor children, that their little hearts should suffer and quail amid these daily horrors of war!

The next evening, about four o'clock, M——'s dear face appeared. He told us that he had heard of all the danger through which we had passed, and was extremely anxious to have us out of reach of the mortar shells, and near him; he also thought we would find our new home on the battle field far superior to this; he wished us to go out as soon as possible. As at this hour in the evening, for the last week, the Federal guns had been quiet until almost sundown, he urged me to be ready in the shortest time possible; so I hastened our arrangements, and we soon were in the ambulance, driving with great speed toward the rifle pits.

O the beautiful sunlight and the fresh evening air! How glowing and delightful it all seemed after my incarceration under the earth! I turned to look again and again at the setting sun and the brilliant crimson glow that suffused the atmosphere. All seemed glad and radiant: the sky—the flowers and trees along our drive—the cool and fragrant breeze—all, save now and then the sullen boom of the mortar, as it slowly cast its death-dealing shell over the life we were leaving behind us.

Were it not for the poor souls still within, I could have clapped my hands in a glad, defiant jubilee as I heard the reports, for I thought I was leaving my greatest fear of our old enemy in the desolate cave of which I had taken my last contemptuous glance; yet, the fear returned forcibly to me afterward.

CHAPTER XVII.

RIDE TO THE FORTIFICATIONS—NUMBER OF CAVES ALONG THE ROAD—APPEARANCE OF THE NEW HOME—CHANGE OF MISSILES.

THE road we were travelling was graded out through the hills; and on every side we could see, thickly strewn among the earthy cliffs, the never-to-be-lost sight of caves—large caves and little caves—some cut out substantially, roomy, and comfortable, with braces and props throughout—many only large enough for one man to take refuge in, standing;—again, at a low place in the earth was a seat for a passer-by in case of danger.

Driving on rapidly, we reached the suburbs of the city, where the road became shady and pleasant—still with caves at every large road excavation, reminding one very much of the numberless holes that swallows make in summer; for both the mortar and Parrott shells disputed this district; and a cave, front in whatever direction it might, was not secure from fragments. M——

impatiently urged on the driver, fearing that when the firing recommenced we would still be on the road. Suddenly, a turn of the drive brought in sight two large forts on the hills above us; and passing down a ravine near one of these, the ambulance stopped. Here we saw two or three of the little shell and bomb proof-houses in the earth, covered with logs and turf. We were hastily taken out and started for our home, when I heard a cutting of the air—the most expressive term I can use for that peculiar sound—above my head; and the balls dropped thickly around me, bringing leaves and small twigs from the trees with them.

I felt a sudden rush to my heart; but the soldiers were camped near, and many stood curiously watching the effect of the sudden fall of metal around me. I would not for the world have shown fear; so, braced by my pride, I walked with a firm and steady pace, notwithstanding the treacherous suggestions of my heart that beat a loud "Run, run." M——, fearing every moment that I might fall by his side, hurried me anxiously along. Within a short distance was the adjutant's office, where we took refuge until the firing became less heavy. Here we found friends, and sat chatting some time.

The "office" was a square excavation made in the side of the hill, covered over with logs and earth, seemingly quite cool and comfortable. I had been confined for so long a time in a narrow space of earth, that daylight, green trees, and ample room became a new pleasure to me. At sundown there was a cessation in the rapid fall of balls and shells; and we again started for our home. I was taken up a little footpath that led from the ravine up under a careless, graceful arch of wild grape vines, whose swinging branchlets were drawn aside; and a low, long room, cut into the hillside and shaded by the growth of forest trees around, was presented to my view as our future home. What a pleasant place, after the close little cave in the city!—large enough for two rooms—the back and sides solid walls of earth, the sloping of the hill bringing down the wall to about four feet at the entrance, leaving the spaces above, between the wall and roof, for light; the side, looking out on the road through the ravine, was entirely open, yet shaded from view by the clustering vines over the pathway.

I took possession delightedly. A blanket, hung across the centre, made us two good-sized rooms: the front room, with a piece of carpet laid down to protect us from the dampness of the floor, and two or three chairs, formed our little parlor; and the back room, quiet and retired, the bedroom. Over the top of the earth, or our house, held up by huge forked props, were the trunks of small trees laid closely across together; over that, brush, limbs, and leaves, and covering all this the thickness of two or three feet of earth beaten down compactly, and thought perfectly safe from Minié balls and Parrott or shrapnell shells.

We had our tent fly drawn over the front, making a very pleasant veranda; for a narrow terrace had been made along the entrance, from which the hill sloped abruptly down to the road in the ravine opposite the dwelling; in the rear the hill rose steeply above us. All was quiet tonight, as it usually is, I was told, when the moon is not brightly shining.

The Federal commanders fear that the Confederates will strive to improve their defences by the moonlight, which is certainly done, firing or not, for the fortifications need constant strengthening, being frequently badly torn by the Parrott shells.

The next morning at four o'clock, I was awakened by a perfect tumult in the air: the explosion of shrapnell and the rattling of shrapnell balls around us reminded me that my dangers and cares were not yet over. How rapidly and thickly the shells and Minié balls fell—Parrott of various sizes—canister and solid shot, until I was almost deafened by the noise and explosions! I lay and thought of the poor soldiers down below in the ravine, with only their tents over their heads; and it seemed in this storm of missiles that all must be killed. How strange so few casualties occur during these projectile storms!

Our little home stood the test nobly. We were in the first line of hills back of the heights that were fortified; and, of course, we felt the full force of the very energetic firing that was constantly kept up; and being so near, many that passed over the first line of hills would fall directly around us.

CHAPTER XVIII.

MORNING—CHARGE OF GENERAL BURBRIDGE—HORRORS OF WAR—AN IMPORTANT DISCOVERY.

How dewy and pleasant the morning! I stood looking out from the little terrace, breathing the fresh air, and learning the new surroundings, so far as my eye went, for it was not safe to venture out from the covering of the cave—the ravine fronting me, shady, dark, and cool—the sun just rising over the hilltop and lighting the upper limbs of the large trees. Up the ravine, the Headquarters, horses were tethered, lazily rising and shaking their coats after the night's rest on the ground— shaking off their drowsiness to begin the breakfast of mulberry leaves. Amidst the constant falling of rifle balls, the birds sang as sweetly, and flew as gayly from tree to tree, as if there were peace and plenty in the land. Plenty there certainly was not in Vicksburg, as any one would have said who had been invited to our little breakfast that morning: bacon side and bread were all; and I had become so accustomed to them, that I obeyed the calls to breakfast with reluctance; eating, most practically, to sustain life, without the slightest relish for the food I was compelled to masticate and swallow.

Yet, all received their trials with cheerfulness. The gentlemen, who breakfasted with us that morning, laughed and made merry over the rations, and told me of the mule meat that was soon to be served up to us.

They were speaking of a charge that had been made, most gallantly, by General Burbridge and the Federal troops of his command, on the Confederate intrenchments: they had rushed over the breastworks and into the rifle pits, driving out the Southern soldiers. The whole Confederate camp near the spot arose in a furious excitement, officers and men alike throwing hand grenades down upon the intruders, until they were forced to retire, after holding the place some little time. I was told that General Burbridge had, laughingly, remarked to a Confederate officer, during the truce, that, staying in the intrenchments in the hot sun, and having hand grenades thrown at him in profusion, was as warm a work as he wished to undertake in one day.

After the Federal troops left the intrenchments, a hole was found in the loose earth of the breastworks that caused much amusement among the Confederate soldiers—a large hole where one of the Federals had literally burrowed his way out from the pits. " I reckon he's some kin to a mole," sagely commented one of the soldiers.

A flag of truce had been sent by the Federal commander, asking leave to bury the killed and remove the wounded that had been left on the field, in one of the charges that had been made on the Confederate lines.

The request had been refused by General Pemberton. Afterward the effluvia from the dead bodies became so intolerable, that he was obliged in his turn to ask a truce, and request the Federal officers to bury their dead. I was distressed to hear of a young Federal lieutenant who had been severely wounded and left on the field by his comrades. He had lived in this condition from Saturday until Monday, lying in the burning sun without water or food; and the men on both sides could witness the agony of the life thus prolonged, without the power to assist him in any way. I was glad, indeed, when I heard the poor man had expired on Monday morning. Another soldier left on the field, badly wounded in the leg, had begged most piteously for water; and lying near the Confederate intrenchments, his cries were all directed to the Confederate soldiers. The firing was heaviest where he lay; and it would have been at the risk of a life to have gone to him; yet, a Confederate soldier asked and obtained leave to carry water to him, and stood and fanned him in the midst of the firing, while he eagerly drank from the heroic soldier's canteen.

The officer who related this little incident had not yet obtained the name of the noble man. Truly, " the bravest are the tenderest; the loving are the daring." How generous—how truly brave the man who would thus dare death! who would, at the risk of life, perform a truly Christian deed! Oh! were all men but true followers of the Prince of Peace, how short would be this warfare! Did only individual Christians strive to do their duty in every respect, this great suffering would not be upon us. There are enough in the world who worship Him who died that all might be happy —enough to stand before the heads of the Christian nation and plead in His name that there be mercy for these dying and bleeding thousands—that these brothers, sons, and husbands may not lie torn, swollen, and writhing in the hot sun, with burning eyes and parched tongues, far, far from those who are powerless to succor them in this fearful time; and, with these pleadings, would ascend prayers to Him who rewards the peacemakers as the children of God—prayers from many an aching, tear-seared heart; and the fierce bitterness, strife, and hatred that move men so, would pale before this blessing. Should they fail, and the wrong go on, then they have done their duty; and they will find mercy, not where the error of man's judgment withholds it, but before Him to whom the least of these are of incalculable value.

One morning George made an important discovery—a newly made stump of sassafras, very near the cave, with large roots extending in every direction, affording us an inexhaustible vein of tea for future use. We had been drinking water with our meals previous to this disclosure; coffee and tea had long since been among the things that were, in the army. We, however, were more fortunate than many of the officers, having access to an excellent cistern near us; while many of our friends used muddy water, or river water, which, being conveyed so great a distance, became extremely warm and disagreeable.

CHAPTER XIX.

AN ACCEPTABLE PRESENT—HUNGER—HALF RATIONS—IN THE RIFLE PITS.

A SERVANT brought me one day a present from an officer, that was acceptable indeed: two large, yellow, ripe, June apples, sealed in a large envelope. They were as much of a variety to me as pineapples would have been.

On another occasion, a gentleman sent me four large slices of ham, having been fortunate enough to procure a small piece himself. Now and then gentlemen in calling would bring to my little girl and myself some little article that it was impossible to procure; and only those who have undergone like privations can understand how truly grateful we felt for these little kindnesses. One day a friend brought us some fruit that had been presented to him. While we were conversing, my little hunger-besieged two-year-old daughter quietly secured it, and, sitting on the floor, ate with avidity. When she had finished nearly all of it, she turned around, with a bright and well-satisfied face, to me, saying, " Mamma, it's so dood!"—the first intimation that I had that my portion had disappeared. Dear child; I trembled for her in the greater trials I believed in store for us. Fruits and vegetables were not to be procured at any price. Every one felt the foreboding of a more serious trouble, the great fear of starvation that stared all in the face causing those who possessed any article in the shape of edibles to retain it for that period to which all looked forward with anxiety—when we would come to actual want.

Already the men in the rifle pits were on half rations—flour or meal enough to furnish bread equivalent in quantity to two biscuits in two days: many of them ate it all at once, and the next day fasted, preferring, as they said, to have one good meal.

So they sat cramped up all day in the pits—their rations cooked in the valley and brought to them—scarcely daring to change their positions and stand erect, for the Federal sharpshooters were watching for the heads; and to rise above the breastworks was almost certain death. Frequently, a Parrott shell would penetrate the intrenchments, and, exploding, cause frightful wounds, and death most frequently. " Ah!" said M——, one day, " it is to the noble men in the rifle pits that Vicksburg will owe aught of honor she may gain in this siege. I revere them, as I see them undergoing every privation with courage and patience, anxious only for the high reputation of the city."

They amused themselves, while lying in the pits, by cutting out little trinkets from the wood of the parapet and the Minié balls that fell around them. Major Fry, from Texas, excelled in skill and ready invention, I think: he sent me one day an arm chair that he had cut from a Minié ball—the most minute affair of the kind I ever saw, yet perfectly symmetrical. At another time, he sent me a diminutive plough made from the parapet wood, with traces of lead, and a lead point made from a Minié ball.

I had often remarked how cheerfully the soldiers bore the hardships of the siege. I saw them often passing with their little sacks containing scanty rations, whistling and chatting pleasantly, as around them thickly flew the balls and shells.

Poor men, yet so badly used, and undergoing so many privations!

CHAPTER XX.

A RAINY MORNING—A WATERSPOUT—DISMAL EXPERIENCE—BRIGHTER PROSPECTS—AN UNFORTUNATE SLEEPER.

THE clouds had been darkening around us all day, and at night we had the prospect of a storm. M—— sent George out with a spade to slope the earth about the roof of our home, and widen the water ditch around it; yet, it was not until the next morning that the rain began falling. By daylight I heard M—— giving orders rapidly about packing the earth firmly, deepening the ditch, and watching the rear of the cave.

I opened my eyes to see without the darkness and gloom of a rainy day—to feel the dampness of the mist upon my face, and to behold M—— standing at the entrance, with the movable articles near him piled out of reach of the driving rain, giving orders to George in regard to our doubly besieged fortress. I lay and listened to the dropping and plashing with a dreamy pleasure at first; but hearing M—— start out to see if all were right, I sprang up, thinking I might assist in keeping out the water. It was a very fortunate move; for I had scarcely begun dressing, when the earth gave away at the head of my bed, and a perfect spout of muddy water burst through the embankment and fell in the centre of the resting place I had so lately left. To run and call M—— to stop the water in the back part of the cave, and, in the greatest haste, to assist Cinth in removing every article that was at all dry, and let the water have free course through, was the work of an instant; yet, in the short time that the water had flowed through the cave, we presented a miserably deluged appearance: trunks were piled on trunks—lines hanging from log to log in the roof, filled with the dripping carpet, blankets, sheets, and miscellaneous articles, dripping with a dreary patter on the floor—chairs turned up together, and packed out of the way—our homelike arrangements all in disorder. And now that the water had been turned that flowed through the cave, I and the servant sat, disconsolately, with our skirts drawn around, and our feet on little blocks of wood to keep them out of the mud, with rueful faces, regarding the sweeping of the water and plashing of rain without.

The water, having overflowed the sides of the ditch, making a new channel, and pouring down at the entrance, had completely washed away our little terrace, leaving a huge and yawning gulf immediately in front of us. I was thus contemplating, sorrowfully, the ruins of our little home, when M—— came down, bringing cheer to us again in the expression of his bright, strong, and calm face; the water was flowing in little streams from his hat down to his coat, flowing over his coat, making little pools on the floor as he stood. He declared that the storm was nearly over, and that we would have some breakfast in spite of it. Taking his hat from his head and shaking the water from it, and from his hair, he bade George take his spade and cut a fireplace near the entrance, bring up his camp kettles, which were full of water, kindle a large fire, and have the breakfast on. He congratulated me upon the perfect safety of our residence, that the water was running around it in regular Venetian style, and that for the present we were perfectly waterproof.

Indeed, our home was in a precarious situation on a rainy day, for we were planted in the bed of the torrent of water that drained from the hill above; yet, M—— assured me that now we had nothing to fear, for with George he had packed the earth perfectly firm and secure. He laughed heartily at my narrow escape; for I declared that I should never have felt in a pleasant humor again if that rush of muddy water had fallen on me.

Soon the fire blazed cheerfully up, and George commenced the preparation of our simple breakfast—M—— going out to attend to some reports. I had always looked forward to the prospect of rain with pleasure, as procuring us some respite from the incessant noise of explosions, and from the whistling and falling of balls. The fury of the storm had scarcely abated, when the tumult and din of the Federal batteries and musketry recommenced; and far from the rain extinguishing the fuse of the shell, there seemed to be an unusually large number falling this morning. I began to feel thoroughly thawed and revived when George set the breakfast on the table and M—— came in; so we sat down quite gayly, in spite of the continued falling of the rain.

The pleasant fire was doing its work, and the earth was rapidly hardening around us.

M—— told me of a colonel of one of the regiments stationed at the foot of one of the fortified hills, who unfortunately slept too long, and the turbulent rush of the waters down the hill broke through all barriers, enveloping him completely in mud, water, sand, and sediment. He sprang from the ground in a towering rage, and could scarcely be persuaded that he was not the victim of a practical joke. So soundly had he slept, that he was entirely oblivious of the storm, and could scarcely believe his rude awakening the work of the elements. M—— told me also, with a grave face, of the poor soldiers he had seen in the rifle pits that morning, standing in water—some with little pieces of carpet drawn around them; others with nothing but their thin clothes, which were saturated; and there they would lie through the day, with only the meal of yesterday to sustain them.

CHAPTER XXI.

**WEARY—THE COURIERS FROM GENERAL JOHNSTON—DANGEROUS PAS-
TURAGE—MULE MEAT—LOCAL SONGS—MISSED BY A MINIÉ BALL.**

I AM told by my friends, who call, that I am looking worn and pale, and frequently asked if I am not weary of this cave life. I parry the question as well as possible, for I do not like to admit it for M——'s sake; yet, I *am* tired and weary—ah! so weary! I never was made to exist under ground; and when I am obliged to, what wonder that I vegetate, like other unfortunate plants—grow wan, spindling, and white! Yet, I must reason with myself: I had chosen this life of suffering with one I love; and what suffering, after all, have I experienced?—privations in the way of good and wholesome food, not half what the poor people around us are experiencing.

A fear of those that can kill the body, and after that have no more that they can do! I will not be unnerved—I have no right to complain. Wherever He hath placed me, there will I be found in His strength; and hereafter I will be brave and steadfast.

To reason with myself in this time of danger was one of the chief employments of my cave life. Time passes on, and all say the siege cannot last much longer; and still we are here—and still the deafening noise of shells—and the variety of missiles that are thrown fall, scattering death in all directions.

About this time, the town was aroused by the arrival of a courier from General Johnston, who brought private despatches to General Pemberton, the nature of which did not transpire; yet, from the very silence of General Pemberton, the officers augured the worst.

The courier brought many letters to the inhabitants from friends without. His manner of entering the city was singular: Taking a skiff in the Yazoo, he proceeded to its confluence with the Mississippi, where he tied the little boat, entered the woods, and awaited the night. At dark he took off his clothing, placed his despatches securely within them, bound the package firmly to a plank, and, going into the river, he sustained his head above the water by holding to the plank, and, in this manner, floated in the darkness through the fleet, and on two miles down the river to Vicksburg, where his arrival was hailed as an event of great importance, in the still life of the city.

The hill opposite our cave might be called "death's point" from the number of animals that had been killed in eating the grass on the sides and summit. In all directions I can see the turf turned up, from the shells that have gone ploughing into the earth. Horses or mules that are tempted to mount the hill by the promise of grass that grows profusely there, invariably come limping down wounded, to die at the base, or are brought down dead from the summit.

A certain number of mules are killed each day by the commissaries, and are issued to the men, all of whom prefer the fresh meat, though it be of mule, to the bacon and salt rations that they have eaten for so long a time without change. There have already been some cases of scurvy: the soldiers have a horror of the disease; therefore, I suppose, the mule meat is all the more welcome. Indeed, I petitioned M—— to have some served on our table. He said : " No ; wait a little longer." He did not like to see me eating mule until I was obliged to ; that he trusted Providence would send us some change shortly.

That very afternoon I was looking out on the opposite hill, where the shells were falling frequently. I noticed a very large, fine cow slowly grazing on the side, and ascending higher and higher as she moved.

It was a matter of wonder with me where she came from, for beef cattle of all kinds had disappeared from Vicksburg. The cow was in fine condition ; and I thought : Poor creature, you are not prudent in eating such dangerous grass. A short time before tea, M—— came up laughing, and said : " Providence has indeed sent you fresh meat, so that you will not have to depend upon mule. A fine cow has been killed by a shell on the opposite hill. The General has taken the meat, and a large share has been sent to you."

I regretted the fate of the animal that I had so lately seen vigorous with life ; yet now, " since fate was so unkind," I gladly received my portion, thinking of the old saw, " it's an ill wind,"

&c. George and some of the boys in the camp cut the meat in strips; and I was able to send sôme soup meat to the courier that rode continually among the shower of balls, and to a poor humped-back soldier, whose strength was giving way from the privation he had undergone: the remainder was rubbed with saltpetre, strung on canes laid across frames, with a slow fire underneath; and the heat of the sun and the fire combined jerked it nicely for future use.

I laughed heartily at the appearance of the cave a day or two after the process. The logs of the roof were hung with festoons of jerked meat, that swung gracefully and constantly above us; and walking around under it, I felt, quite like an Indian, I suppose, after a successful chase, that starvation for a while was far in the background.

It was astonishing how the young officers kept up their spirits, frequently singing quartets and glees amid the pattering of Minié balls; and I often heard gay peals of laughter from head-quarters, as the officers that had spent the day, and perhaps the night, previous in the rifle pits, would collect to make out reports. This evening a gentleman visited us, and, among other songs, sang words to the air of the "Mocking Bird," which I will write:

> " 'Twas at the siege of Vicksburg,
> Of Vicksburg, of Vicksburg—
> 'Twas at the siege of Vicksburg,
> When the Parrott shells were whistling through the air
> Listen to the Parrott shells—
> Listen to the Parrott shells:
> The Parrott shells are whistling through the air.
>
> " Oh! well will we remember—
> Remember—remember
> Tough mule meat, June *sans* November,
> And the Minié balls that whistled through the air.
> Listen to the Minié balls—
> Listen to the Minié balls:
> The Minié balls are singing in the air."

Songs of every description are composed in honor of narrow escapes, unlucky incidents, brave deeds, &c.; songs—humorous, pathetic, and tragic—are sung in every manner of voice. Sometimes hoarse, with surprising loudness and depth; again, with richly modulated tones and much soft volume and melody—all sing, according to differently accustomed tastes.

I heard, one night, a soldier down the ravine singing one of the weird, melodious hymns that negroes often sing; and, amid the firing and crashing of projectiles, it floated up to me in soft, musical undertones that were fascinating in the extreme: the wailing of the earthly unrest—the longing for the glorious home that the warm imagery pictures to be glorious in golden lights and silvery radiance—of song and brilliant happiness! The voice was full and triumphant. Then the rapid change, in low and mournful cadence, to the earth, the clay, the mire—to death, to suffering, to sin! " I wonder, Lord, will I ever get to heaven—to the New Jerusalem?" came with the ending of every verse. I bowed my face in my hands. Yes! heaven was so far off! Yet—" he that cometh to me, I will in nowise cast out "— our grasp is firm, but our eyes are blind. Some day, after the earthly longings are stilled, we will know the exceeding glory.

Though singing songs of every description, yet how often we are made to feel that any moment the summons may come!

I was sewing, one day, near one side of the cave, where the bank slopes and lights up the room like a window. Near this opening I was sitting, when I suddenly remembered some little article I wished in another part of the room. Crossing to procure it, I was returning, when a

Minié ball came whizzing through the opening, passed my chair, and fell beyond it. Had I been still sitting, I should have stopped it. Conceive how speedily I took the chair into another part of the room, and sat in it!

CHAPTER XXII.

A WOUNDED HORSE—SHRAPNELL SHELLS—CHARGE ON THE INTRENCH-
MENTS—FEARFUL FIRING.

ONE evening I noticed one of the horses tied in the ravine, acting very strangely—writhing and struggling as if in pain. One of the soldiers went to him and found that he was very badly wounded in the flank by a Minié ball. The poor creature's agony was dreadful: he would reach his head up as far as possible into the tree to which he was tied, and cling with his mouth, while his neck and body quivered with the pain. Every motion, instead of being violent, as most horses would have been when wounded, had a stately grace of eloquent suffering that is indescribable. How I wanted to go to him and pat and soothe him! The halter was taken off, and he was turned free. Going to a tree, he leaned his body against it, and moaned, with half closed eyes, shivering frequently throughout his huge body, as if the pain were too great to bear.

Then, turning his head entirely around, he would gaze at the group of soldiers that stood pityingly near, as if he was looking for human sympathy. The master refused to have him shot, hoping he would recover; but it must have been evident that this day was the last of his strong, proud life: the noble black was doomed. After the gentle faithfulness of his service, it was cruel to prolong his suffering: after the simple meals of mulberry leaves, with scarcely sustenance enough to maintain life, why should this pain and agony be permitted to rack his already weakened body? These truths were set aside, and the master looked with pity; yet, it seemed, a selfish pity.

Becoming restless with the pain, the poor brute staggered blindly on. And now my eyes fill with tears; for he has fallen, with a weary moan, between the banks of the little rivulet in the ravine, his head thrown on the sod, and the bright, intelligent eye turned still upon the men who have been his comrades in many a battle, standing still near him.

Poor fellow!—those low and frequent moans

and trembling limbs tell them that death has stricken you already—that you are far beyond human sympathy. In the midst of all the falling shells, cannot one reach him, giving him peace and death? I see an axe handed to one of the bystanders, and turn suddenly away from the scene. The quick, soft stroke! I know it must be over. Again I look, and the glossy, black body is being taken out from our sight, to be replaced by new sufferings, and to be forgotten in new incidents.

There is one missile, were I a soldier, that would totally put me to rout—and that is a shrapnell shell. Only those who have heard several coming at a time, exploding near, and scattering hundreds of small balls around them, can tell how fearful the noise they make—a wild scream—a clattering and whizzing sound that never fails in striking terror to my heart! It seemed sometimes that as many as fifty balls fell immediately around our door. I could have sent out at any time, near the entrance of our cave, and had a bucketful of balls from shrapnell and the Minié rifle, picked up in the shortest possible time.

One old, gray-headed, cheerful-hearted soldier,

whom I had talked with often, was passing through the ravine for water, immediately opposite our cave. A Minié ball struck him in the lower part of the leg; he coolly stooped down, tied his handkerchief around it, and passed on. So constantly fell projectiles of all descriptions, that I became almost indifferent to them. Only the hideous noise of numerous shrapnell could startle me now. Generally at four o'clock in the morning the shrapnell were thrown more furiously than at any other time through the day. At about seven, the Minié balls began falling, accompanied by Parrott, canister, solid shot, and shrapnell shells; and through every minute in the day this constant play of artillery and musketry was kept up from the Federal lines. General Pemberton had ordered the Confederate batteries to remain silent, unless particular orders were given to fire, or an assault was made on the works.

One afternoon I remember so vividly! One of the surgeons of the staff was chatting with M——, when I heard a rushing and peculiar sound, as if some one were rapidly cutting through the air, near and around me, with a sword

Both the doctor and M—— sprang to their feet, as the sound grew more confused, seeming as if the sudden rush of a volume of water was pouring down the hill. I saw M—— turn to the doctor and say: "They're coming!" I dared not ask any questions; yet, I at first supposed the intrenchments were taken. M——, without a word, drew on another coat and threw the linen one he had worn to me, with a laugh. I suppose I must have looked rather wild; for I could not tell or imagine the meaning of the confusing and singular noise around us. Taking his sword, M—— started immediately. I feared every moment that he would fall, for the balls fell like hail. I turned to the doctor, questioning: "Are they coming over the hill?" He laughed, and said:

"Oh! no; they are only making a charge on the intrenchments; and the rushing in the air you hear is the numerous small balls flying over us."

The strange, bewildering sound lasted for some time. The doctor soon took his leave, saying that the wounded would be brought in for him to attend. I sat for half an hour hearing the constant rushing and surging around me, and the quick dropping of balls; the ground trembled from the frequent discharge of the Confederate cannon What was likely to be the result, I could not tell; for the ravine below, lately so full of animation,

seemed to be totally deserted, save now and then the rapid gallop of a courier through the shower of balls along the road. Soon there came a gradual cessation, quieting more and more down to the old interval of a minute between the discharges; soon M—— came home, reporting one or two wounded and one killed. It seems miraculous to me that, amid such a shower of balls, so few persons should be injured.

CHAPTER XXIII.

AN UNHAPPY ACCIDENT—THE UNFORTUNATE LADIES OF VICKSBURG—APPROACH OF MORTAR SHELLS NEAR THE INTRENCHMENTS.

A FEW days after the assault on the Confederate fortifications, a sad accident cast a gloom over all the little community encamped in the ravine—officers, soldiers, and servants: A soldier, named Henry, had noticed my little girl often, bringing her flowers at one time, an apple at another, and again a young mocking bird, and had attached her to him much by these little kindnesses. Frequently, on seeing him pass, she would call his name, and clap her hands gleefully, as he rode the general's handsome horse for water, causing him to prance past the cave for her amusement. She called my attention to him one morning, saying: "O mamma, look at Henny's horse how he plays!" He was riding a small black horse that was exceedingly wild, and striving to accustom it to the rapid evolutions of the Texas troops, turning in his saddle to grasp something from the ground, as he moved speedily on. Soon after, he rode the horse for water; and I saw him return and fasten it to a tree.

Afterward I saw him come down the hill opposite, with an unexploded shrapnell shell in his hand. In a few moments I heard a quick explosion in the ravine, followed by a cry—a sudden, agonized cry. I ran to the entrance, and saw a courier, whom I had noticed frequently passing by, roll slowly over into the rivulet of the ravine and lie motionless, at a little distance: Henry—oh, poor Henry!—holding out his mangled arms—the hands torn and hanging from the bleeding, ghastly wrists—a fearful wound in his head—the blood pouring from his wounds. Shot, gasping, wild, he staggered around, crying piteously, " Where are you, boys? O boys, where are you? Oh, I am hurt! I am hurt! Boys, come to me! —come to me! God have mercy! Almighty God, have mercy!"

My little girl clung to my dress, saying, " O mamma, poor Henny's killed! Now he'll die, mamma. Oh, poor Henny!" I carried her away from the painful sight.

My first impulse was to run down to them with the few remedies I possessed. Then I thought of the crowd of soldiers around the men; and if M—— should come and see me there—the only lady—he might think I did wrong; so I sent my servant, with camphor and other slight remedies I possessed, and turned into my cave, with a sickened heart.

In a few moments, the litters pass by, going toward the hospital, the blood streaming from that of Henry, who still moaned and cried " for the boys to come to him," and " for God to pity him."

But the other bore the still, motionless body of the young courier, who, in the strength of his life, had been so suddenly stricken. It seems that the two men had been trying to take out the screw from an unexploded shell for the purpose of securing the powder; in turning it, the fuse had become ignited, communicating the fire to the powder, and the fatal explosion ensued.

Henry had been struck in the head by a fragment—his hands torn from his arms; one or two .ragments had also lodged in his body. The courier had been struck in two places in his head, and a number of balls had entered his body. Poor soldier! his mother lived in Yazoo City; and he was her only son. So near was she, yet unable to hold his head and set the seal of her love on his lips ere the breath fled from them forever! He lived until the sun went down, speaking no word—making no moan; only the quickly drawn breath told that life still flickered in the mangled body. Henry died, also, that night, still unconscious of the sorrowful comrades around his bed—still calling on God to pity him.

After the bodies of the wounded men had been carried away, we heard loud wailings and cries in the direction of the city. I was told a negro woman, in walking through the yard, had been struck by a fragment of shell, and instantly killed. The screams of the women of Vicksburg were the saddest I have ever heard. The wailings over the dead seemed full of a heart-sick agony. I cannot attempt to describe the thrill of pity, mingled with fear, that pierced my soul, as suddenly vibrating through the air would come these sorrowful shrieks!—these pitiful moans!—sometimes almost simultaneously with the explosion of a shell. This anguish over the dead and wound ed was particularly low and mournful, perhaps from the depression. Many women were utterly sick through constant fear and apprehension. It is strange that the ladies were almost constantly in caves, and yet, did one go out for a short time, she was almost certain to be wounded; while the officers and soldiers rode and walked about, with very little destruction of life ensuing.

An officer was telling me of two soldiers near his camp, who had been severely wounded by Minié balls—one shot through the hand and lung; the other through the side.

A new cause for apprehension came to me about this time: the mortar boats were endeavoring to throw their bombs as far as the intrenchments, and almost succeeded. I could see them at night falling near the opposite hill; and I was in a constant state of trepidation, lest they should be cast still nearer us. After witnessing the brilliant streams of light that they created in the heavens, one night, and feeling repeatedly thankful that they always fell short of the hill we inhabited, I gradually grew sleepy in utter loneliness, for M—— seldom finished receiving reports until eleven. I wearily turned to the little mattress on the floor, said my prayers, and retired. I had been sleeping some time, for the moon was shining brightly, when I was awakened by loud cries and screams : " Where shall we go ? Oh ! where shall we go ? " My immediate conclusion was that some woman had been killed or wounded, as every now and then I could see the mortar shells dropping on the hill opposite. I therefore thought that I had been spared in Vicksburg, as long as I reasonably could hope, from the variety of changes through which I had passed ; and immediately I was seized with a severe panic. If shells had not been falling from the battle field also, I fear I should have started in that direction—so great was my dread of the mortars !—and run, I cared not where, out of their range.

But the counter awe of Parrott shells kept me where I was. I sat up in bed in a fearful state of excitement ; called M—— again and again, without the slightest response ; at last, a sleepily uttered " What is the matter ? " gave me an opportunity of informing him that we would all be killed, and telling him, while the cold moisture of fear broke out over my forehead, that the mortar shells were nearer than ever, and that the next one would probably fall upon our cave. Awakened at last to my distressed state of mind, and hearing me say that I knew some woman had been killed, he got up, dressed, took up his cap, and went out to see what had happened, telling me he would return shortly—looking back, laughing as he went, and saying to me that I was fearfully demoralized for so good a soldier. He soon returned, telling me that a negro man had been killed at the entrance of a cave a little beyond us, toward the city; that his mistress, wife, and the young ladies of the family were very badly frightened, having taken refuge in the adjutant's office.

CHAPTER XXIV.

DEATH OF A FAITHFUL SERVANT—BLOWING UP OF A FORT—LOSS OF PROMINENT OFFICERS—SURRENDER OF VICKSBURG.

THE next day, the family were invited up to our cave; and the lady told me, with tears, of the death of the faithful old man, who had served her mother before her. The morning of the day he died, he called her to him, and said: " Mistess, I feel like I ain't gwin' to live much longer. Tell young master, when you see him, that I've been praying for him dis day; tell him it smites my heart mightily to think I won't see his young face dis day with the childern. Please tell the young folks, mistess, to come; and let me pray with them." " Oh! uncle!" the mistress answered, " don't talk that way; you will live many years yet, I hope." The young ladies were called, and knelt, while he prayed for them and all he loved, shaking hands with them, and speaking to each one separately, as they left. His cave was next his mistress's. That night he sat smoking his pipe near the entrance, when a mortar shell, exploding near, sent a fragment into the old man's side, rending it open, and tearing away his hip. He lived a few moments, and was carried into the cave. Turning to his mistress, while he shook his head, he said: "Don't stay here, mistess. I said the Lord wanted me." And so the good old Christian died. When he had breathed his last, a sudden panic seized them, for shell after shell fell near them; and they all ran. Some of the gentlemen, hearing them cry, brought them to headquarters.

The next day, the news came that one of the forts to the left of us had been undermined and blown up, killing sixty men; then of the death of the gallant Colonel Irwin, of Missouri; and again, the next day, of the death of the brave old General Green, of Missouri.

We were now swiftly nearing the end of our siege life: the rations had nearly all been given out. For the last few days I had been sick; still

I tried to overcome the languid feeling of utter prostration. My little one had swung in her hammock, reduced in strength, with a low fever flushing in her face. M—— was all anxiety, I could plainly see. A soldier brought up, one morning, a little jaybird, as a plaything for the child. After playing with it for a short time, she turned wearily away. "Miss Mary," said the servant, "she's hungry; let me make her some soup from the bird." At first I refused: the poor little plaything should not die; then, as I thought of the child, I half consented. With the utmost haste, Cinth disappeared; and the next time she appeared, it was with a cup of soup, and a little plate, on which lay the white meat of the poor little bird.

On Saturday a painful calm prevailed: there had been a truce proclaimed; and so long had the constant firing been kept up, that the stillness now was absolutely oppressive.

At ten o'clock General Bowen passed by, dressed in full uniform, accompanied by Colonel Montgomery, and preceded by a courier bearing a white flag. M—— came by, and asked me if I would like to walk out; so I put on my bonnet and sullied forth beyond the terrace, for the first time since I entered. On the hill above us, the earth was literally covered with fragments of shell—Parrott, shrapnell, canister; besides lead in all shapes and forms, and a long kind of solid shot, shaped like a small Parrott shell. Minié balls lay in every direction, flattened, dented, and bent from the contact with trees and pieces of wood in their flight. The grass seemed deadened —the ground ploughed into furrows in many places; while scattered over all, like giants' pepper, in numberless quantity, were the shrapnell balls.

I could now see how very near to the rifle pits my cave lay: only a small ravine between the two hills separated us. In about two hours, General Bowen returned. No one knew, or seemed to know, why a truce had been made; but all believed that a treaty of surrender was pending. Nothing was talked about among the officers but the all-engrossing theme. Many wished to cut their way out and make the risk their own; but I secretly hoped that no such bloody hazard would be attempted.

The next morning, M—— came up, with a pale

face, saying: " It's all over! The white flag floats from our forts! Vicksburg has surrendered!"

He put on his uniform coat, silently buckled on his sword, and prepared to take out the men, to deliver up their arms in front of the fortification.

I felt a strange unrest, the quiet of the day was so unnatural. I walked up and down the cave until M—— returned. The day was extremely warm; and he came with a violent headache. He told me that the Federal troops had acted splendidly; they were stationed opposite the place where the Confederate troops marched up and stacked their arms; and they seemed to feel sorry for the poor fellows who had defended the place for so long a time. Far different from what he had expected, not a jeer or taunt came from any one of the Federal soldiers. Occasionally, a cheer would be heard; but the majority seemed to regard the poor unsuccessful soldiers with a generous sympathy.

After the surrender, the old gray-headed soldier, in passing on the hill near the cave, stopped, and, touching his hat, said:

" It's a sad day this, madam; I little thought we'd come to it, when we first stopped in the intrenchments. I hope you'll yet be happy, madam, after all the trouble you've seen."

To which I mentally responded, " Amen."

The poor, hunchback soldier, who had been sick, and who, at home in Southern Mississippi, is worth a million of dollars, I have been told, yet within Vicksburg has been nearly starved, walked out to-day in the pleasant air, for the first time for many days.

I stood in the doorway and caught my first sight of the Federal uniform since the surrender. That afternoon the road was filled with them, walking about, looking at the forts and the headquarter horses: wagons also filled the road, drawn by the handsome United States horses. Poor M——, after keeping his horse upon mulberry leaves during the forty-eight days, saw him no more! After the surrender in the evening, George rode into the city on his mule: thinking to " shine," as the negroes say, he rode M——'s handsome, silver-mounted dragoon-saddle. I could not help laughing when he returned, with a sorry face, reporting himself safe, but the saddle gone. M—— questioned and requestioned him, aghast at his loss; for a saddle was a valuable article in our little community; and George, who felt as badly as any one, said: "I met a Yankee, who told me: 'Git down off dat mule; I'm gwin' to hab dat saddle.' I said: 'No; I ain't gwin' to do no such thing.' He took out his pistol, and I jumped down."

So Mister George brought back to M—— a saddle that better befitted his mule than the one he rode off on — a much worn, common affair, made of wood. I felt sorry for M——. That evening George brought evil news again: another horse had been taken. His remaining horse and his only saddle finished the news of the day.

The next morning, Monday, as I was passing through the cave, I saw something stirring at the base of one of the supports of the roof: taking a second look, I beheld a large snake curled between the earth and the upright post. I went out quickly and sent one of the servants for M——, who, coming up immediately, took up his sword and fastened one of the folds of the reptile to the post. It gave one quick dart toward him, with open jaws. Fortunately, the length of the sword was greater than the upper length of body; and the snake fell to the earth a few inches from M——, who set his heel firmly on it, and severed the head from the body with the sword. I have never seen so large a snake; it was fully as large round the body as the bowl of a good-sized glass tumbler, and over two yards long.

CHAPTER XXV.

A FRIGHT—GEORGE MY PROTECTOR—A POLITE SOLDIER GETS THE TENT FLY.

In the afternoon, M—— went into the city, with some of the officers, to make arrangements for me. I was much amused, though I did not let them see it, as they set off on their poor mulberry-fed horses. M—— had been presented by some one, after the loss of his horse, with a little, lame, subdued-looking animal, to whom food of any kind seemed a rarity; and the poor horse ambled along as if he considered his weight a great affliction. Our whole little household had been drawn out to witness the departure of the brilliant (?) cavalcade.

Afterward, as I sat with a book at the entrance, I heard steps, and, looking up, I saw a large, burly negro, with a most disagreeable face, dressed in Federal uniform, and armed, coming up the little path that led to the cave. As he advanced toward me, I sprang to my feet; but George, who was luckily near, crossed over from the "sassafras bed," carving knife in hand, with which he was digging some of the root. Standing between us, he said: "Where are you gwin', old man?" "None your business," he returned, pausing a moment. I was just on the point of calling for some of the gentlemen at headquarters, when he turned and went round the cave on the hill. "I'll make dis knife show you what's your business," growled George. Poor George! he had been my faithful defender throughout all my vicissitudes in Vicksburg.

Soon after, George came to me in a great state of excitement, and said: "Oh! Miss Mary, a Yankee soldier was just going with our tent fly from the top of the cave, and I made him stop and leave it." A Federal soldier came down the side of the hill, stopped, and took my little daughter's hand and said some pleasant words to her; turned to me, touching his hat, with a smile, and said, "Good morning." I bowed in return, while a lucky thought came to me: Here was a kind-hearted, polite soldier; why not let him take the tent fly, in the place of some undeserving man? So I said: "Soldier, would you like a tent fly?" He answered: "Oh! yes, madam; I would like one very much." So I sent George to get it for him. He expressed himself very grateful—disliked to take it, fearful of robbing us; but I assured him he was welcome; so he again bade me good morning, and carried off his acquisition.

The Confederate troops were being marched into Vicksburg to take the parole that the terms of the treaty of surrender demanded. In a few days they would leave the city they had held so long.

On Friday they began their march toward the South; and on Saturday poor George came to me, and said he had put on a pair of blue pants, and, thinking they would take him for a Federal soldier, had tried to slip through after M——, but he was turned back; so he came, begging me to try and get him a pass: the effort was made; and to this day I do not know whether he ever reached M—— or not.

Saturday evening, Vicksburg, with her terraced hills—with her pleasant homes and sad memories, passed from my view in the gathering twilight — passed, but the river flowed on the same, and the stars shone out with the same calm light! But the many eyes—O Vicksburg!—that have gazed on thy terraced hills—on thy green and sunny gardens—on the flow of the river—the calm of the stars—those eyes! how many thou hast closed on the world forever!

LETTERS

OF TRIAL AND TRAVEL.

LETTERS.

GAYOSO HOUSE, MEMPHIS, *April*, 1862.

MY DEAR J——:

I am just in from dinner; and you would be amused to see the different faces—I might as well say the different appetites; for the Army of Missouri and Arkansas have been undergoing rigorous fasts of late; and the little episode of the battle of Elkhorn and the consequent privations have helped not a little the gaunt appearance of these military characters. All eat, eat rapidly; from General V—— D—— down to the smallest lieutenant, whose manner of playing the epicure over the different dishes ordered, is a study. The confidential consultations with the waiter over them, together with the knowing unconsciousness of bestowing his small change, almost convinces me that he is a brigadier-general, or a colonel, at least. You see streaming in constantly this tide of human beings, to eat, stare at the ladies, talk, and order much wine in the excitement of military anecdotes; for you must understand that a civilian is a "rara avis" amid the brilliant uniforms of the dining room. Yet, amid all this mass and huge crowd, the majority are polished gentlemen, who have evidently seen much of the world, and who are men of purpose and character.

General V—— D—— and staff sit not far from me—looked at rather jealously by the Missourians, as ranking and commanding them over their favorite general. Yet, he always treats the old general with the utmost consideration and courtesy. On the other side sits General P——, with his kind, benevolent face. The poor old gentleman finds at the table his lightest reserves become his heaviest forces: nearly all his staff are about him.

And, as I sit half amused at the expression of some faces, and thinking deeply of the mute, yet determined impress of character on others, two gentlemen come in—one in plain citizen's clothing, with heavy black beard and high forehead—with stooping gait and hands behind him. I am told he is Governor J——, of Missouri. His face puzzles me—it is thoughtful and singular. By his side, with tall, lithe, slender figure, fully erect, walks General J—— T——. You will scarcely think it possible that this is the so-frequently talked of J—— T——. I thought him an ordinary man, did not you? Yet, this is anything but an ordinary man. The keen dark eye sweeps the room as he enters, taking us all in at a glance— a quick, daring, decisive, resolute face. I can make nothing more out of him. Yet, there is more of thought and intellect than you see at first. He is dressed in full uniform, with sword and sash, and has quite a military air.

There are many Saint Louisians here; you see them scattered around the tables quite plentifully. General C—— is among the number. He sits at some distance, and looks quite worn and sad. You know—do you not?—that he is the father of young Churchill Clark, who was killed at Elkhorn. Have I ever told you his history? It is this: He graduated at West Point in the commencement of the war; and knowing and having a great admiration for General P——, he joined him at once: he was put in command of some artillery; and showing himself a youth of courage and ability—for he was only twenty years old—his command was increased. Throughout the constant trials and sufferings of the campaign, he showed himself equal in courage, daring, and judgment, to many older heads. He was particularly beloved by General P——. At Elkhorn, as ever, his battery sustained itself with coolness and bravery. As the general rode by, he said some cheering words to young Clark, who took off his cap and waved it, saying, " General, we will hold our own," or words to that effect, when a ball sped from the enemy, and crashed in the young, ardent brain as he spoke.

I have been told that the general was affected to tears. He knelt by his side, vainly seeking for some trace of the strong, young life, but the pulses were stilled forever; and Churchill Clark lay a stiffened corpse in the long, wet grass at Elkhorn. And so his father sits silent and alone, and all respect the grief that none can assuage.

In a few days we leave. The gentlemen all go to Corinth, where a battle, in all probability, will take place before long. Fort Pillow can hardly hold out, under the daily bombardment that we hear from the gunboats; and if it falls, Memphis, on taking leave of the Confederate officers, will usher in the Federal to quarters in the Gayoso.

Adieu.

Memphis, *April.*

Dear J——:

Again I write you from the Gayoso House, which still teems with Missourians, and many ladies—some few from St. Louis. General P——'s parlor is filled with ladies from morning until night. I have been told that on one occasion some ladies, who were the reverse of beautiful, were coming in to see him, when he turned to one of his staff officers, and told him that it was his duty to assist him—that here was an opportunity: he must kiss these ladies for him; but the officer was politely deaf until too late.

It is astonishing to see how ladies do flock to see the old general; and all kiss him, as a matter of course. I rode out to the camp of the Missourians with M——, a few mornings since. It is pleasantly situated near the bank of the river. The men seem to be in good spirits; although moving them across the Mississippi has been an unpopular act. The poor fellows are being taken out to Corinth as fast as transportation can be furnished them. The compliment is paid them of being placed in the most dangerous position;

for we daily expect an attack from the Federal forces on Corinth.

Would you like to see those you love complimented in this way? You can form no idea of the love and devotion shown by the Missouri troops for their general. I happened to be standing near a window at the end of the hall, last evening, as some regiments passed by the Gayoso on their way out to the depot, bound for Corinth. General P—— stood out on the veranda as they passed by, and shouts and cheers for the old general and Missouri rent the air.

General J—— T—— called on me this morning, and amused me much with some of his adventures in Missouri last winter; among others, he told us of his dash into the little town of Commerce for food. His men were ordered to take a certain amount, lay down the money, and leave. As he sat on a small horse, waiting for them, out came the "heroine of Commerce," as he called the lady. I have forgotten her name; yet, I think it was O'Sullivan. She walked up to the general, shook her clenched hand in his face, and told him he was a robber and a scoundrel. Her husband pulled her by the arm and tried to make her desist; but she was deaf to his entreaties, standing part of the time on one side of the little horse, and part of the time on the other; first, shaking her clenched hand at him, and then standing, with arms folded, calling him all manner of names. Some of the officers wished General T—— to have her confined to her own house until his departure; but he laughed, and said: "No; let her alone." She still continued hovering around him, threatening and talking.

He said: "Oh! Mrs. O'Sullivan, you are a modest woman—a very modest woman. Madam, don't you think your house stands in need of you?" Powerless fell the irony: wherever he went, he was followed by the persistent Mrs. O'Sullivan; stop where he would, Mrs. O'Sullivan was by his side, much to the amusement of his followers; go where he would, up rose Mrs. O'Sullivan unexpectedly at corners — red-faced and bitter—always in the same belligerent, defiant state.

A steamboat was seen coming down the river. General T—— ordered his men to hide behind a woodpile until it came up, expecting to get supplies from it. When they thought themselves disposed out of sight, General T—— raised his eyes, and behold! some little distance up the river, stood the inevitable Mrs. O'Sullivan, violently gesticulating to the boat, and crying, " Turn, turn ! J—— T—— is here ; " at the same time waving her apron and sun bonnet, in quite a frantic manner. The boat turned indeed; and although the scheme failed, behind the woodpile sat General T——, chagrined at the failure, yet laughing most heartily at the attitude and *mal-à-propos* appearance of Mrs. O'Sullivan.

The hotel is crowded with military men : many wounded at the late battle of Shiloh, going around with arms in slings ; others supported by crutches. The ladies are seemingly having a very gay time : the halls are filled with promenaders, and the parlors with gay young couples, music, and laughter.

Yet, a sudden surprise has come to all : New Orleans has fallen—an unexpected blow to most of the Southern officers. I cannot but think, as I see all the life and bustle around me, of the different scenes a week or two hence, when the fearful battle of Corinth will have taken place. How many that are now happy and full of life, looking forward with confidence to the laurels that may be won, before the struggle is over will be silent forever in death! or, worse, perhaps lamed and maimed for life! General Beauregard's works are said to be fine; yet, the Federal approaches are said to be greatly superior.

My husband goes to-morrow to Corinth; and I will go to O——, Miss., to await the result of what all seem to think will be a most bloody struggle. I will write on reaching O——; until then, farewell.

O―――, *May 1st.*

THE expected battle has not yet come off, and I am still awaiting the result; busying myself about many things, visiting and returning visits from my old friends; dividing my time between the world and the hospital, the lights and shades of life. Ah, the shades! My dear J―――, you can little imagine how much suffering I have witnessed in the last few weeks—how much, that acts or kind words have no power to mitigate. There have been many wounded brought in from Corinth, many who have died since their arrival, many who will die; but, saddest of all, a young boy, too young to be a soldier, yet possessing all a soldier's spirit. I walked into a ward, one morning, that I had visited the evening before—a ward of very sick patients—and saw an old man sitting by a new cot, fanning a young boy, who lay with flushed face, and burning eyes fixed on the ceiling. As I advanced toward them, the weather-bronzed man stood stiffly erect, making me a quaint, half-awkward, military salute, saying, as he did so, "My boy, ma'am!" "Is he wounded?" I asked. He threw back the sheet that covered him, pointed to the stump of a limb amputated near the thigh: "He has gained the cross," he said, while his head grew more erect, as he held back the sheet with the fan, and his eye shot out the grim ghost of a smile.

A proud, iron soldier the man was, I could see. The boy was delirious; so I shall tell you of the man. Refusing to be seated as long as a lady remained standing in the room, he stood stiffly upright at the head of the cot, keeping each fly from the face of the boy with the tenderness of a mother. A limp brown hat was on the side of his head, shading his eyes, that followed me in all parts of the room. A red cord and tassel hung from one side of his hat, and gave him a jaunty air that was quite out of keeping with the quaint stiffness of his manner. After speaking to the sick and wounded soldiers around, asking after their wounds and wants, I returned to the young boy's cot, and heard the old man's story. Don't be weary if I give it to you; he had so much pride in his boy, let that be my extenuation.

"We belong to the Texas Rangers, ma'am, the boy and me; he could ride as well as the rest of them, ma'am, a year ago. When the war broke out, and we practised regularly like, he was the best rider in the company—could pick anything he wanted off the ground as he was going. He's only fourteen, ma'am—a fine-grown lad, indeed. His mother was the likeliest woman I ever seed," with a deprecating bow to me; "he's got her eyes —the finest eyes God ever made, she had, ma'am. She died when quite young like, leaving him to me, a little shaver, and he's been by me ever since. The boys and me tried to overpersuade him out of the army; 'peared like he was too young for such business; but he wouldn't hear to it, not he, ma'am, and here he is," passing his sleeve across his eyes.

"Well, ma'am, so he staid with us; and when we got to Corinth, General Beauregard offered a cross of honor to the ones that showed themselves the best soldiers. So our boys talked a heap about who'd get it; but this boy says nothing. Well, one day we were ordered out to scout, and we came up with the Yankees, and we fit 'em a half hour or so, when I seed this youngster by my side kind adrooping by a tree, but standing his ground. Well, we routed them at last, when I found the boy's leg was all shattered, and he'd kept up like nothing wan't the matter. So when we went back to Corinth, it got noised about like from the soldiers to the officers—how he'd held out. And, more'n all, the time when his leg was being cut off, we couldn't get any chloroform, morphine, or the like: he just sit up like a brave lad, and off it went, without a word out of him. So the doctors they talked of that; and he's been notified that he'll get the first cross, and the boys'll be monstrous fond of him, and feel most like they'd got it themselves. If he'd get rid of his fever and pick up like, I'd be a happy man," he said anxiously.

Pardon me do I tire you; but let me take you to visit the sick prisoners. The old man that we pass in the hall, with his arm and leg in a frame, will never recover; yet he does not know it, and frequently asks me if I think he will get a pension when he is well, if he loses his leg and arm. He persists in keeping his face covered with a handkerchief, raising it up and peeping out, if he hears my voice, each day, with his usual salutation: "You've come, have ye?" If I bring any little article of food that I think the patients will relish, this old man must be fed by me, and I am frequently amused at the directions he gives me, for he is extremely practical and particular : " Now, if you will turn the spoon a little to one side, I will turn my mouth in this direction, and the custard will pass safely in." Poor man, without a friend, both arms badly wounded, and leg shattered, dying by degrees, yet to the last the handkerchief would be raised, and the cheery welcome greet me, " Ye're come, have ye?"

I think I can see you looking around in this ward to learn which are the prisoners, for all seem cheerful and talkative. In this cot by the door, with a wounded limb in a frame—like a huge lion —lies a man, large whiskered, large bodied, and long limbed, yet with a pleasant smile of greeting as we enter and make our inquiries after his wound. He is "better this morning, thank you," or, "I am obliged to you, not quite so well." A little picture on the table by his side, of a child three years of age, is never closed. A little child, blue eyed, with bare white neck, and plump round arms, showing the mother's wish that the picture should be fair and lovely to the father's eye. The Federal flag is on the cover. The man, a captain, is of an Illinois company. The child and mother, with tearful eyes and wistful hearts, look over the wide expanse of land and water that separates, over the cruel bounds that man has set—still faithful in their love. Still watching, and hoping, for the time when liberty will be his, and he, constant and true, will return to them. He tells me the name of the little one, with a sorrowful look at me with his dark eye. If he is free, if he ever sees these words, he will remember how the little one was gazed on by a lady in deep mourning, to whose heart a child of three years brought a sad and tearful memory.

Come to the next cot with me; do not shrink from this blackened brow. Yesterday this was a noble-faced, gray-haired, old Confederate soldier, with the plaintive, lovely smile of perfect resignation. He suffers much from a wound in his body; seldom talks, yet always smiles gratefully for the slightest attention. This morning I find the erysipelas has broken out, spreading over his forehead and a part of his face. He cautions me, with the same pleasant, resigned smile, about coming near him, lest I take the disease. The blackened skin is from the effect of iodine to stay its progress. He will not live: dear, patient old man, my heart aches for him, yet I can give him nothing but kind words.

This morning I brought the men in this ward toast. The old man slept, and I gave to each his portion. Engaged in talking to a prisoner in another part of the room, I heard the Illinoisian say: "Let me divide this toast with you; I do not need it all." I turned, and heard the old man reply: "Oh, no; you keep it." I procured his toast and brought it to him, laughingly telling the prisoner I believed I saw the dawn of the millennium.

Do you not wish, dear J——, that the dawning was indeed with us; that brave and noble men should no more suffer, bleed, and die, but live; and in their lives grow more thankful and worthy of the Divine blood that has been shed for the removal of the fearful suffering and warfare that is all around us?

Pardon me for the length of time I have detained you, and remember me as ever, dear J——,
Yours.

O———, *June*, 1862.

CAN you credit it, dear J———, General Beauregard has evacuated Corinth? You have learned it by this time through the papers, and share with me the surprise. Our feelings have fluctuated with the news from Corinth for weeks. First, an engagement would probably ensue the following day. Then, some one had heard heavy guns, and was sure that the battle had taken place. And the next day, all quiet at Corinth. But the most astonishing of all, for we were prepared for everything besides, Corinth has been left quietly; absolutely left, and the Federal troops probably occupy the place. Every one has something to say on the subject, and all are more brilliant in their ideas for the reason that all have full scope to exercise them. No one possesses reliable information, and we are a conjecturing community—gentlemen as well as ladies. Something out of the common order of affairs, you will say.

But a truce to politics, of which I am very fond, and, like most women, know very little about. Why should a woman of sense care to talk about anything but dress and her servants? So I attended a pleasant little *soirée* a few evenings since, graced by the fair and elegant daughters of General P——, of Tennessee, and the young bride of Jacob J——'s only son, a sweet young girl. All were in full evening dress, though the guests were few.

But a novelty, listen: A young Spanish bride—a brilliant woman—dazzled my eyes for the evening. Conversing only in her beautiful national language, she with animated gestures fascinates and enlightens one readily in relation to her themes. Then she warbles most beautifully, and one can scarcely complain that her higher notes lack in power, as she rises from the instrument, placing her hand on her heart, saying brokenly the only English words she is mistress of: "Oh! pity me, pity!" with an arch reverence to her audience.

I am troubled about our poor hospital patients, the one third of whom you have not met with me, each has a separate individuality that interests me exceedingly. It is feared that the Federal troops will advance on O——, and the patients will be removed to a safer place below. I will be sorry to see them leave, poor fellows. The boy that gained a double cross at Corinth has closed his eyes softly and calmly. Suffering will never disturb him more. He is dead. The old man has gone back to his company with spasms of pain in his heart, of which the world will never know.

Let me tell you of the man's devotion. The boy's fever still raged, with slighter and slighter intervals. The medicine failed to procure the desired effect. The physicians looked anxious as they approached his cot. I wanted to take the old man's hand and tell him of the Friend in heaven, from whom death itself can never separate us; but a foolish fear withheld me. One night the physicians met around the little cot, the old man, as usual when others were near, standing stiffly at the head, yet, with alarmed and burning eyes, intently reading each face. A sad reading, hopeless—the eyes told that, while the hand sought the faintly beating pulse. "Doctor, may I try to save my boy my own way?" said the old man, following the physician into the hall. "Yes, do as you choose with him, only do not give him unnecessary pain."

In the morning a large tub of cold water was taken to the ward and placed by the sick boy's cot; and, to the dismay of the soldiers in the beds around, the boy was lifted out, wounded as he was, by the strong and gentle arms of one in whose eyes he was more precious than the rarest of diamonds and gold. A quick douse, and he was rubbed well, covered closely, and soon slept soundly, the perspiration breaking out profusely for the first time in two days. He was decidedly better, and the proud smile on the father's face was a happy thing to see. Gradually he grew more feeble, the fever returned, and one morning, with an aching heart, I saw the calmness of death in the closed eyes and motionless nostril. Standing at the head of the bed, his hat drawn over his eyes, his arms folded in a stern and patient agony, the father stood watching yet, most faithfully. I cannot express to you the grief that my sympathy brought—the grief, and constantly the words : " Alone! all alone! 'My boy! oh, my boy!"

The ladies wished to have a large funeral over the brave, young soldier ; but the physicians would not consent to having him buried in town, saying that the soldiers were all worthy of attention, and that no distinction could be allowed. So, before he was buried, I went out to the hospital and looked my last on the young, dead face, from which all trace of suffering had fled: only peace and rest now forever!

Pain and anguish were making a deep impress on the face of the man by the head: the drawn lines of watching and suffering were more evident, as with a strained smile, and almost a gasp of pain, he thanked me for the interest I had taken. "Everybody is so kind!" he said. He had gone into town that morning and purchased a little black coat, placing it on the small form. A black velvet vest, white bosom, and the cravat tied over the white, boyish throat, told of the tenderness that shrank not from the coldness of death.

"He's like his mother, ma'am, more than ever, now," he whispered, softly drawing the sheet over the inanimate form; and turning squarely around, with his back to me, I saw him draw again and again his sleeve across his eyes. We are born to this human sorrow; and yet it is an appalling thing to me. You have expressed an interest in these visits to the wounded and dying; therefore I speak.

One more life that hovers over the grave! —one more who has suffered, oh, I cannot express to you how much! A prisoner from Iowa, belonging to the second Iowa cavalry, was captured at Farmington, near Corinth, shot through the body so badly, that very little hope was entertained of his recovery: he lingered some weeks, and dwindled from a robust, hearty man, down to a poor emaciated being—seldom talking—never complaining, yet suffering much, I could see.

When I came, one morning, the ward master whispered aside to me that he had been dying through the night. I entered the ward; his eye sought mine, with a wistful look, and brightened as I came near his bed. I smoothed the hair from his forehead, moistened his lips, and then, taking the fly brush, resolved to stay by him to the last. Oh, dear J——! those wistful eyes that followed every motion of mine!—those anxious, dying eyes!

What was the poor mother doing now, of whom he whispered to me? How little she knew that the eyes that were so dear, now were looking their last on the light! Far away from home and friends, among strangers, the soul was swiftly passing out into the great sea of eternity, the bright hopes of which so softly regulate this life-tide of ours!—passing out—passing out, with a lingering look of unfathomable speech, into my face; for my face told him what my lips faltered in doing!

"If I can write to your mother before you are free, what shall I say?"

"You know," he whispered.

"You are very sick, and God may not spare your life; will you say one little prayer after me?" And so a few words were said, that, with long pauses, he whispered after me, almost gasping at the last word. And thus beside him I sat, the gaze from his eyes into mine growing more and more intense. It seemed as if his whole soul was drawn out in unutterable language. At length, the quivering eyelid, the softly fleeting breath, ebbing out—yes, ebbing out so swiftly!

O Father! give this tried soul thy rest, through thy dear Son.

Free at last, prisoner! Peace to thy soul! God grant his peace!

My friend, do you dread death? I have seen it come so often as a relief from pain and distress, that I could not but bless it. Do not forget that you asked for these details; and believe, as I wish you always to, in my affection, Yours.

It is long since I have heard from you, dear J——; long since I have written. You will notice that I am again at O——. Soon after writing my last, the Federal troops took possession of Holly Springs and threatened O——. The hospital patients were removed; and I crossed the country to meet my husband, who was at Tupelo. After spending some time in Pontotoc, I continued on to Tupelo, and for some time remained on a plantation six miles distant. Meantime the battle of Iuka occurred; and the loss of the brave General Little was deeply felt by the Missourians. The troops returned in dejection. Shortly, they were marched across to Ripley, where a junction was formed with the troops under General V—— D——; and an attack was made on Corinth, in which the troops behaved gallantly, but all to no purpose: a complete repulse it proved; and the army under the two generals narrowly escaped capture.

The wives and families of the officers were, of course, distressed and anxious. Couriers daily came galloping into the town, with the most conflicting reports.

At one time we heard that the Missourians were completely cut to pieces; again, that they were all captured. One of the couriers said he had seen my husband lying in an ambulance as he passed. How much distressed I was, you can imagine. Yet, two days passed wearily along; and still no tidings. The evening of the second day, as I sat in the moonlight on the portico, I heard a vehicle coming down the road with great speed; as it neared the house, I saw that it was an ambulance. My worst fears now took shape and form: M—— wounded, perhaps mortally wounded, I thought; and I ran swiftly down the walk. The driver met me at the gate, telling me that he had been sent with all speed after me— that Tupelo would be evacuated during the night, and my husband had written to the post quartermaster, placing me in his charge. I also had a letter. The quartermaster would take me over the country with the wagon train at daylight in the morning. My husband was well, he answered to my first, earnest inquiry.

It was now nine o'clock; my little daughter was in bed sleeping soundly. The man, a sergeant, who was well known to my husband, had, as yet, not supped; so, while he ate, I gathered my baggage together, wrapped a shawl around my sleeping child, and then, with a hurried good by, we drove off, six miles through the woods, through what had been an impassable swamp. Now the gloom of the huge trees brought to my mind all the thrilling tales I had heard of travellers being waylaid in swamps and dense woods. I looked at the shadows on the trunks of trees, and imagined a man skulked in the darkness behind them. The owls were crying mournfully, and the plaintive song of the whippoorwill came to us from the dense recesses of the forest.

My servant crept closely to my side, for negroes, in their vivid imaginations, fill the woods at night with phantoms and ghosts of the departed. Frequently, after detailing the events of the recent battle to us, our driver, in the full moonlight, would break the silence with one of the stirring camp airs, whistling loud and shrilly; then my martial and political hopes would rise; but as we would again plunge into the darkness of the rugged cypress trees, where the owl and whippoorwill vied with each other, a silence would again come over us, and I again become a timid, fearful woman.

Soon we saw lights through the trees, then the rows of camp fires, and noise and bustle became the prominent features of the town: cattle were driven through, with many a shout and halloo; wagons were passing rapidly; soldiers were cooking rations at the camp fires—a scene of busy preparation.

We drove to the quartermaster's office, and the gentlemen conducted us in, regretting that they had been obliged to send for me in such a summary manner. The order to move had come at dark; and since then they had been employed constantly, as the town must be evacuated by daylight; for the Federal forces were advancing rapidly.

The house was an unfinished building: one large, long room comprised the second story, with a small portion partitioned off, and dignified by the name of office. To this I, with my servant, was conducted through piles of mule collars, harness, bridles, &c.

Here I was glad to find a little camp cot, on which I laid my child for the first time out of my arms. With many apologies for the poor accommodations they had to offer me, the gentlemen took their leave; and I could hear the quick orders to clerks, drivers, and soldiers, as they recommenced their hurried preparations. I took my knitting and sat by the window. The moon was low in the heavens; yet the tumult continued throughout the town. My child slept peacefully—her father many miles away, yet, I knew, filled with anxiety for our welfare.

At dawn we were on our way. The first night, I slept in Pontotoc at a friend's house. The gentlemen camped out of town about a mile. In the morning, before I had left my room, my friends called and left a message for me with the lady of the house. I was to start as soon as I could, and strive to gain the head of the wagon train, thereby escaping the dust. Our driver was a soldier from Arkansas—a quiet, mild, little man, with very little force. We drove on briskly in the pleasant morning air for two or three hours, and saw nothing of the train: perhaps we were before them. Presently, we stopped and held a consultation. In every opinion that I expressed in regard to the matter, I found a ready echo from the little man, pro and con. We had driven perhaps too rapidly: no signs of the wagons could we find. Waiting patiently for a time, a disagreeable foreboding crossed my mind. I had not been told which road to take; there were two: perhaps we were on the wrong one. O—— was forty miles from Pontotoc; we had already gone nine, and could not now return expecting to find our friends.

The only alternative was to drive through to O——, where M—— designed meeting us. So, in answer to the little man's query, "Don't you think we'd better whip up and try to make O—— by night?" I said, "Yes." Clouds began to overspread the sky; and I heard mutterings of thunder in the distance; still the sun shone out fitfully; and I hoped the rain would not fall near us. Driving on with speed, we had proceeded but a few miles, when the unmistakable evidences of a storm, that would soon burst upon us, convinced me that a shelter must be sought; where, it was hard tell, for the road we travelled was almost destitute of houses. I was in despair, as the wind whistled around us, driving in eddies the leaves and dried grass about the ground, and swaying high and low, with a moaning sound, the limbs of the huge forest trees. In my anxiety, I grasped at a straw. I remembered, in travelling this road before, that M—— had pointed out a by road through the woods, that led to Lafayette Springs. The proprietor knew my husband; and I resolved to take a country road that I saw leading in the direction I imagined the Springs to be. Picture me, J——, if you can, sitting up in the centre of the ambulance, my servant by my side, little J—— between us—the little driver, meek and resigned, turning when I said turn, stopping when I said stop. Taking a strange road, I knew not where, we drew near, at last, a most unpromising-looking cabin, the inhabitants of which filled the door at the sound of wheels—in every variety of size—robed in yellow dresses, surmounted by tangled white heads. The old lady " knew thar was some springs somewhar abouts, and reckoned this road might run thar;" then, resuming her pipe, looked for confirmation of the statement to her eldest daughter, who said : " Yes, she reckoned, the road would take us thar, if we kept ' straight ahead.' "

" Whip the mules," I cried, " and drive rapidly;" for the storm was darkening around us; and the ambulance jingled a chorus through the silent "piny woods." Large drops were now falling; the wind moaned and surged mournfully through the "barren," moaned and swept over the narrow road, whirling the "pine points" as we passed; faster and faster fell the rain. Our heavier clothing, shawls, cloaks, &c., were with the trunks: one light shawl, in which I enveloped my child, was all we possessed in this emergency. The ambulance cover was dotted with bullet holes, through which the rain dropped in cold relentlessness. The little driver was suffering martyrdom: drawn up as closely as possible, with his blanket around him, the wind driving the rain in sheets between him and the mules, he looked to me in the mist like an inanimate, round, brown ball. Soon, the floor of the ambulance filled so rapidly with water, that he threw his blanket over the top of the conveyance to keep the rain from falling through; then subsiding again, the only sign of life about the little being was the mechanical process of whipping the mules.

A little side road presented itself, leading into the forest, freshly marked with wagon tracks. Hearing the barking of a dog not far distant, I **ordered** the driver to turn in search of a house.

Proceeding a quarter of a mile, we came to another little cabin. Through the rain, the weak voice of the little driver brought to the door a woman, who informed us that Lafayette Springs were three miles on " ahead." Highly elate, the little man turned to me, and, with a glad face, saying, " Very good news," whipped up his mules; and I firmly believe the man was nearsighted; for in two minutes more we would have gone off a precipice that was almost hidden by the tops of trees that grew far below at the base. " Stop!" I cried, as the heads of the mules were almost over the verge of the cliff. The little man meekly asked what he should do. " Back the mules!" I cried; and, after a troublesome detention, we at last turned and found ourselves on the road again. " We like to had a right smart time thar," said the little man to me. " We did, indeed," I returned, blandly; for I feared I had hurt the poor man's feelings in speaking so quickly at that critical time. Gladly we reached the Springs through the driving rain, and were pleasantly welcomed. The landlord did all that he could for my comfort.

I had the pleasure of meeting a friend who

had met my husband, and who told me much about the recent battle. The next morning, we started early. I determined, although it was a raw, disagreeable morning, to be done with my lonely wanderings. We had gone about four miles, shivering in the dismal mist, when I heard a quick galloping along the road. The curtain of the ambulance was lifted—a blithe good morning in a voice I could not mistake : M—— was riding by our side, asking how on earth we had contrived to wander so far off from our friends. I could answer nothing to this bantering. Corinth, with all its bloody horrors that have been so vividly before my mind, the constant anxiety I had felt, and now my tribulations were ended— M—— in person here to take charge of us! I covered my face and cried like a silly child. Do not blame me; you have never been lost in the woods in a storm, and felt that the responsibility of every action rested with you. M—— had been sent on business to Pontotoc--had heard of us there and followed, fearing that we might have met with some accident I will accompany M—— in a few days to Holly Springs, where Generals P——, V—— D——, and L—— are intrenching with their forces. As I write, the sunlight fades away; and only the fading crimson light lies across my paper. In closing, let me entreat you to remember always, as you read, my affection for you,

As ever.

HOLLY SPRINGS.

You wished me to keep a journal for you, dear J——; but I answered that a journal would be a dull compound of dates, with three lines setting forth the vapidity of most days; and I would rather write events as they passed. You replied that my letters must be voluminous if they were satisfactory. Do you not already repent the remark? I rejoice, if length is pleasing, my letters are satisfactory.

The battle of Corinth was a bloody failure. Oh the blood that has flowed in this wonderful and most appalling warfare!—the tears and the suffering! Can there be nothing done to assuage the fierce passions of men? Oh! J——, could you see, as I have, the torn and mangled human beings brought from the field of battle, with loud cries to God for death!—for mercy and for death! —you, like me, would ask anxiously, " Can nothing do away with this death?—this anguish? Can no appeal be made by which peace may come to us?" But woman weeps, while man strikes!

Holly Springs, with its white verandahed houses, its pleasant gardens, wide streets, and hospitable homes, is the most pleasant of Southern towns; though crowded and teeming with soldiers and officers.

The inhabitants seem uniting in the efforts to entertain. Generals V—— D——, P——, L——, and T—— have each their respective headquarters in the town. A week ago I attended a review of the troops under Generals L—— and T——. They presented a fine appearance: most of them were newly uniformed and renovated from their prison clothing. General V—— D——, who is called the finest horseman in the army, galloped up and down the line on a fleet, beautiful black horse, followed by General P—— on a large bay that galloped heavily and with less speed.

There were many ladies present on horseback, scattered around the field, with generally a gay group of officers surrounding them. Day before yesterday we rode out to a large review of the Missouri troops under General P——. There were spectators from the whole country around: many came up on the cars from a distance. Such imperishable renown have the Missouri troops gained in the late battle of Corinth, that all are anxious to witness their review, and cheer the brave fellows who have suffered so much. Although driven back and obliged to retreat, their gallant struggle over two rows of superior fortifications in the face of a galling fire, the Southern people will never forget.

General P—— is greatly beloved by the people also; though the heads of the Government are strongly opposed to him. It is natural, of course, that President Davis should suppose a regularly educated military man would be more likely to understand the science of war than a man who had not made it his study. But why does he cripple so efficient an officer as General P—— certainly is, so as almost to render him inefficient?

The Missourians on review looked fresh and lively. General P——, attended by his staff, stood near us in the pause, while we waited the arrival of General V—— D——. One of General P——'s staff officers started across the field to carry a despatch, when his horse, stumbling, fell on the grass, rolling the brilliantly uniformed gentleman over and over on the sod, much to the amusement of the spectators, who cheered him lustily. I felt sorry for him; and although some of his friends were talking to me at the time, I could scarcely conceal a smile. But the men, who, half a mile distant, have been drawn in line, now wheel, form, and march around the little hillock in the distance. See, the sun glances on the bayonets of the guns, as they ascend, and in coming down over the brow of the hill, the regular swing of the line and glance of the steel show the discipline they have been under.

Now they pass by the general, who sits a little behind General V—— D——, and near General L——. Among the artillery, I saw the Lady Richardson, captured and brought away from Corinth. As they come on, and pass by General V—— D——, they salute; which is answered by his raising his cap to the colors, disclosing a proud, youthful head, surrounded by curls. He is immediately before me, and I do not see his face, which is marked with deep lines I have noticed before. In the evening, after the review, I attended a party given to the generals here collected. The house was crowded; the generals, with their staff and other officers, were there, and some of the lovely ladies of Holly Springs. The supper was handsome. Toasts were drunk to Generals P—— and V—— D——, and all went merry, &c. But in the midst of a conversation, an officer told me that the Federal forces were advancing on Holly Springs, and that probably the Confederate forces would evacuate the town in a day or two. So, dear J——, there is no telling where I will be when I write next.

JACKSON.

I KNOW you are smiling, as you see Jackson written at the head of my letter—smiling to think how systematically I have bowed myself out of one town after the other, as the Federal troops have bowed themselves in; yet you know the old saw, "He that fights, and runs away," &c.; though I can take no comfort in this, as fighting has been my abomination since the war began. I have always, in peaceful times, had an admiration for heroes in brilliant uniforms, and would now, if the hero could possibly assure me that the brilliant uniform would always be filled with life. But how can one feel a pleasure in the gilt trappings of a friend, when they know that they may possibly serve as an anxiously sought target for some sharpshooter. You do not wonder at my quotation in favor of a retrograde movement in this frame of mind, do you? For the last week or two I have passed from one state of excitement to another, so that I am glad indeed to find a quiet resting place.

From Holly Springs the army under Generals V—— D—— and P—— retreated to Abbeville, where they remained stationary for a time. One day the inhabitants of O—— were alarmed by the distant booming of cannon. A great excitement prevailed, and various rumors went the rounds. One that the Federal troops had reached the Tallahatchee; another that they had crossed, and a battle was progressing between the Federal and Confederate forces.

The town grew wide awake. Wagons passed and repassed. Numerous families were seen walking rapidly toward the depot, carriages filled with ladies and children driving swiftly in the same direction. My friends were preparing to leave also. I had received a telegram from M——, telling me to be in readiness to take my departure during the afternoon. My preparations were made. A gentleman came on the down train to accompany me, when, to our great disappointment, passengers were not allowed to go on the train, for the hospital patients were all to be taken off before passengers could be accommodated. My friend was, however, by particular favor, allowed to ride in a baggage car with my trunks. The next day, Sunday, how little it seemed like the Sabbath! passenger trains were to run if the stores could all be transported. So a number of friends, with myself, took our seats quite early in the cars at the depot, and waited patiently hour after hour, hearing most distracting rumors, until my patience had become nearly exhausted.

In the afternoon, great was my joy on seeing M—— enter the car. The army was retreating from Abbeville. Our friends resolved to take their carriage and cross the country to Columbus. M—— said he could get an ambulance for me, but I would be obliged to keep up with the army, as the Federal forces were following closely. The cars were vacated quickly, and I saw the last of my friends. An ambulance came up, and I was soon riding rapidly southward. That night we stopped at a roadside house. During the next day the greater portion of the army passed by, and encamped below the house we were in for the night.

The next morning was gloomy, dark, and disagreeable. While I waited for M—— to come with an ambulance, Gen. P—— invited me to ride with him. The roads were in the most miserable condition, and for a time we drove on a corduroy road.

Just imagine me, dear J——, on a corduroy road, jolting through a swamp, with my child in my arms; the general talking in the calmest and most urbane manner. Yet the gloom of the day was over me, and I felt dismally miserable. Soon the rain began to pour down. We were at this time on the high road, which became every moment worse, from the travel of the artillery, the greater portion of which was before us. Immediately behind the general's ambulance drove the carriage of a lady, who had been compelled, like myself, to abandon the cars.

How incessantly the rain poured down! Now and then the ambulance would drive on the side of the road, stopping to let the infantry pass. Poor fellows! wet and begrimed with mud, plodding with blankets and knapsacks strapped on their backs, and guns on their shoulders; troublesome accompaniments at any time—far more so now in the driving rain. At the foot of the hills we would frequently be obliged to halt, sometimes for an hour, awaiting the passage of the artillery over the brow of the ascent. The Federal troops were close in the rear. The horses strained and pulled, but the mud was so deep and heavy that the wheels became clogged, and I looked anxiously up, expecting to see some huge cannon, impelled by its weight, return to the base of the hill. Frequently the soldiers would be obliged to wade through the deep ruts of mud on the hillside, and give a new impulse to some wavering piece, assisting the horses, and pushing the weighty gun-carriage with united strength.

In the rain sat the staff officers on their dripping horses; and, giving orders from the ambulance window, the old general urged on the men. I wondered at the patience, the kindness with which he spoke to all; rapidly and cheerily to the staff officers: "Ride on, and see what obstructs the road;" and in a tone of sympathy, through the rain, to the straggling soldier: "Keep up, men, keep up." "We camp near, do we?" he called out in clear tones to the inspector. And the men raised their drooping heads and pressed forward at the encouragement in the well-known voice. I see the power of kindness with these men, dear J——. There are few general officers in the Confederacy so well-beloved by their men as

General P——, yet he is only kind and perfectly just.

That night we stopped beyond Water Valley, at a house where the poor hostess tried to make us comfortable, and gave us much of her company, telling us that she was " cousin to Stonewall Jackson's wife and Hill's wife; " but she " reckoned they did not know it, and wouldn't think much of it, if they did." She brought in a large baby, and sat down by the general's side, telling him that she was going to name that baby after him. The general was as affable as usual; but I frequently turned to the window to conceal my amusement.

Suddenly I was startled by her turning quickly to me, and asking if I " would ever think her any kin to Stonewall Jackson's wife and Hill's wife." Never having seen either of the above-named ladies, I conscientiously answered I did not know as I should.

Wakened by the bugle call the next morning, I hastily arose, and in a few moments was ready to depart. We had proceeded but five miles when an aid-de-camp rode up, and told General P——

that General Pemberton wished him to return to Water Valley immediately, as the Federal forces were quite near, and the Confederate soldiers must make a stand. We alighted and sat a few moments in a negro cabin. Then the general mounted and rode toward Water Valley, followed by his staff officers. The lady and myself proceeded on with the wagons beyond Coffeeville, where the train halted and prepared to camp for the night. As yet I had not heard from M—— since he rode off with the general, and I scarcely knew what to do. The soldiers were thrown out on picket duty around the train; as a Federal force was also to the left of us, near the little town of Charleston. Heavy skirmishing was going on at Water Valley, we were told. As no house was near, the gentleman who had charge of the lady and myself told us that he would put up a pleasant tent, and make us quite comfortable. So a tent was pitched on a little hillock near, and I rested comfortably during the night. Early in the morning we were on our way, the remainder of the army having come up. At length we reached Grenada in safety, yet sorely pressed by the Federal troops.

Thus you see, dear J——, that I am unlucky enough to be identified with some retreat or threatened city. From Memphis, or over the greater distance that separates us, we can span our love; and through all, I am

Yours.

THE END